WITHDRAWN FROM STOCK

NUMBER ON CODE LABEL.

HARGED
IN

RDUE BOOK
AMAGE T
EP

KU-591-575

THE
IRISH TRADITION

THE
IRISH TRADITION

BY

ROBIN FLOWER

OXFORD
AT THE CLARENDON PRESS

Oxford University Press, Ely House, London W. 1

GLASGOW NEW YORK TORONTO MELBOURNE WELLINGTON
CAPE TOWN SALISBURY IBADAN NAIROBI DAR ES SALAAM LUSAKA ADDIS ABABA
BOMBAY CALCUTTA MADRAS KARACHI LAHORE DACCA
KUALA LUMPUR SINGAPORE HONG KONG TOKYO

FIRST EDITION 1947
REPRINTED 1948, 1963, 1966, 1970

019815 2035

COUNTY LIBRARY
TOWN CENTRE, TALLAGHT

ACC. NO.   0198 152035
COPY NO.   TC 1009
INV. NO.   BACKSTCK
PRICE IR£ 6.00
CLASS   891.62

Re-Bound...... 1.00

PRINTED IN GREAT BRITAIN

CONTENTS

PREFACE

WHEN in 1945 Dr. Flower felt that he would never be able to write the history of Irish literature he had long planned, he decided on the advice of his friends Professors J. H. Delargy and Myles Dillon to publish a selection he had put together of what he had already said or written on the subject on various occasions over a long period of years. He was already too ill to revise and annotate the manuscript himself and he turned to friends and colleagues for help. The references in this book—except in Chapter V, where nearly all the notes are his own, are due to the kindness of Mr. David Greene. Help has also been given by Professor Eleanor Knott and Mr. Gerard Murphy. The main work of preparing the manuscript for the press has been generously undertaken by Professor Myles Dillon, and Dr. D. A. Binchy has revised the proofs.

As Dr. Flower intended, his Sir John Rhŷs Memorial Lecture for 1927, *Ireland and Medieval Europe*, has been incorporated in Chapter V by kind permission of the Secretary of the British Academy, and part of the introduction to Professor T. F. O'Rahilly's *Dánta Grádha* (2nd edition, 1926) has with his permission been inserted as Chapter VI; where in that introduction Irish poems were cited in the original, Professor Dillon has substituted Dr. Flower's own translations published in *Love's Bitter-Sweet* (Cuala Press, 1925), and in *Poems and Translations* (Constable, 1931).

A large part of the book covers the same ground as the Donnellan Lectures which Dr. Flower delivered at Trinity College, Dublin, in 1938.

We should like to express our gratitude to all those who have thus made it possible to publish the book.

IDA M. FLOWER
BARBARA FLOWER

I

THE FOUNDING OF THE TRADITION

A VISITOR to Ireland familiar with Gaelic literature has
his attention arrested everywhere in that beautiful
island by many features, natural and artificial, which set
him searching among his memories and clothing hill and
river, rath and church and castle, with the lively and intimate colouring of long-descended tradition. And if he
yields himself to the spell of that lure of recollection and
summons back out of the past the kings and saints and
scholars and poets whose names still cling about the places
that they knew, he may be contented to recall that he is
acting in the very spirit of those devoted scholars to whom
that tradition owes its origin and survival. For the poets
of Ireland cultivated with an unremitting assiduity a study
to which they gave the name *dindshenchas*, the lore of the
high places, until by the accretion of centuries there came
into existence a large body of literature in prose and verse,
forming a kind of Dictionary of National Topography,
which fitted the famous sites of the country each with its
appropriate legend. It was one of the obligations of a poet
to have this knowledge ready at call, and if faced by a
demand to relate the associations of some deserted rath
or lonely pillar-stone he failed to render an exact and
credible account, he was shamed to the very roots of
his being.

An early text, edited by Miss Knott,[1] gives us a clear
picture of this function of the poets in action. It will appear
later that the southern part of the County Antrim and the
neighbouring portion of the County Down was an active
centre of historical study in the sixth and seventh centuries.

[1] *Ériu*, viii. 155.

B

And it is here that the scene of our tale is laid, in the fort of Mag Line, the seat of the kings of Ulster at that period.

Eochu Rígéices was the chief poet of Ireland. Fiachna mac Boetaín was ever desiring him to come to make poetry for him, for Fiachna was king of Ulster and Eochu was of the Ulidians. 'I will not be in your company,' said Eochu, 'of all the kings that are in Ireland, for there is a young lad with you, Mongán son of Fiachna. And that is the lad that is most of knowledge in Ireland, the evilly disposed will be setting him to contend with me, I shall put a curse on him, and that will be a matter of strife between thee and me.' 'Not so,' says Fiachna, 'I will speak to my son that he contend not with thee, he shall be the most courteous to thee of all my household.' ' 'Tis well,' says Eochu, 'so shall it be done and so shall be to a year's end.' He was there one day relating matters of knowledge. ' 'Tis ill done of thee, Mongán,' said the serving lads, 'not to cross the clown that speaks a lie.' ' 'Tis well,' says Mongán. Fiachna went on his royal visitation with Eochu in his company. As they were going the way one day they saw six mighty pillar stones in front of them and four novice clerics about the stones. 'What make ye there, clerics?' says Fiachna. 'We are here in quest of knowledge and information; God has brought to us the King poet of Ireland, to wit Eochu, to make clear to us who planted these stones and in what manner he set them in array.' 'Well,' says Eochu, 'I have no recollection of that. Methinks 'twas the Clanna Dedad that raised them for the building of the castle of Cúroí.' 'Good, Eochu,' said one of them, 'the novice clerics declare that thou art gone astray.' 'Blame him not,' says another. 'Perchance he is in ignorance,' says his fellow. 'Well,' says Eochu, 'and you, what is your interpretation of them?' 'This is our information: there are three stones here of a champion band and three of a warrior band. 'Twas Conall Cernach that set them, together with Illand son of Fergus that slew three men here in his prentice fight. He was unable to rear the stones being so young, and Fergus aided him to lift them, for it was a custom of the men of Ulster that, wherever they should perform their prentice deed of valour, they raised pillar stones to the number of the men they slew; and now begone, Eochu, with thy ignorance.' 'Be not shamed, Eochu,' says Fiachna, 'the clerics are a good match for thee.'

The story continues in the same way. Eochu fails to read the secrets of the two great raths and is mocked by the young clerics. They return home and the tale goes on.

Mongán was with his people in the house when they came. ' 'Tis well,' says Eochu. 'Thou, Mongán, hast done this thing, well I know.' 'Thou hast said it,' says Mongán. 'Thou shalt have no good of it,' says Eochu. 'I will leave a blemish on thee in requital of it. Thou hast made great sport for thyself and thou shalt be without sport because of it. Thou shalt have no issue but horseboys, thou shalt leave no great inheritance after thee.'

This whole story, its place and persons and motive, is significant. The question concerns the historical traditions of certain places, the persons of the debate are a famous poet, a learned princeling, and a company of young clerics, and. the place is that Pictish kingdom of Dalaradia which had taken over the traditions of the ancient Ulidia, the themes of ancient saga. There is still no suggestion of a written record; it is a contest of rival memories. The poet is that Eochu Rígéices who has been identified with Dallán Forgaill, leader of the poets whom St. Columcille saved from exile, who composed the riddling elegy of the saint. We shall perhaps be justified in assuming that in some such environment our written tradition began.

The old Irish society was organized upon an intensely aristocratic basis, and, like all aristocratic societies, set great store by those memories of past achievement which feed the pride and enhance the prestige of a dominant class. The function of the poets was to keep alive this long-descended record in its full detail of genealogy and varied incident. It was inevitable that, when this mnemonic tradi-

tion met the Latin tradition of writing, it should be fixed in
the new form which offered a greater guarantee of per-
manence. The kings and the poets and the clerics worked
together to this end. So in the *Senchus Mór*, 'The Great
Tradition', the central compilation of the ancient Irish law,
it is claimed that king and saint and poet co-operated to
draw up the consecrated code. And there the relation
between poet and cleric is clearly set down:[1]

> Now until the coming of Patrick speech was not suffered to
> be given in Ireland but to three: to a historian for narration
> and the relating of tales; to a poet for eulogy and satire; to a
> brehon lawyer for giving judgement according to the old tradi-
> tion and precedent. But after the coming of Patrick every
> speech of these men is under the yoke of the men of the white
> [blessed] language, that is, the scriptures.

The name *fili*, 'poet', originally with a wider meaning
'seer', comprehended all these functions of the men of learning in pre-Christian Ireland, and it was to them that the
monastic historians of the sixth and seventh centuries had
recourse for all those memories of the past which they
desired to put on record in their new medium of writing.
These men of the new learning set themselves from an early
date to consider how the Irish history which they had
received from their predecessors, vivid in detail, but regret-
tably loose in chronology, might be fitted into the scheme
of universal history which ruled in the Latin church. Professor Eoin Mac Neill has shown us how they set about
their task.[2] This scheme had been laid down once for all
for Christians in the *Chronicle* of Eusebius as translated and
continued by St. Jerome and Prosper of Aquitaine. The
theory at the basis of this remarkable compilation was that
the great world kingdoms—Assyria, Egypt, Palestine,
Greece—had all by a divine providence led up to the
Roman Empire which, in its turn by the peace of the

[1] *Ancient Laws*, i. 18.   [2] *Celtic Ireland*, 25 ff.

Church under Constantine, had become the Empire of Christ and had given the world constitution its final form. The actual arrangement of the *Chronicle* corresponded to this conception. The whole history of the ancient world was set out in a series of parallel columns, one for each kingdom, and the events of each kingdom were synchronized so that the advance of history, century by century, could be followed at a glance for each kingdom and for all the kingdoms. It was a simple matter to add another column for Ireland, but much less simple to settle the chronology so that the Irish kings might appear in a due succession and in a right relation to their contemporaries in the great world kingdoms. The monks set themselves to the task with an heroic ardour and, by methods which Procrustes might have envied, successfully achieved their complicated labour of synchronism. That they set great store by the method which achieved this curious fabric of history may be deduced from the fact that the favourite word for a historian in Irish at this time was *fer comgne*, 'a synchronizer'. Once the process was completed by the columnar method of Eusebius and Jerome, they abandoned this schematic arrangement and reduced the whole fabric to the form of consecutive annals. A chronicle formed in this manner lies at the base of all the older Irish monastic annals, and there is reason to believe that it was already in existence in the early seventh century.

The language was still Latin except, of course, for the Irish names, but it is plain from the entries relating to Irish history that much of the epic material which has come down to us in texts of a later date was already in existence, though exactly in what form it would be hazardous to conjecture. By the seventh century the monks had accepted the pagan tradition and put it on one level with the historical material which came to them under the sanction of the fathers of the Church, who themselves had received it from the written tradition of Israel, Greece, and Rome. There was, admittedly, no written tradition in ancient Ireland. It was desperately necessary to give a validity to the oral tradition upon which they depended for the Irish events of their chronicle. How was this to be done? It has often been imagined since the advent of wireless telegraphy that those vibrations which are our voices, once surrendered to the air, never come to rest but wander about for ever in the ether as potentialities of sound. Thus, it is argued, if only an appropriate machinery could be devised and the wavelengths of the innumerable periods of the past be established, we might listen in to history and eavesdrop upon all that part of action which is committed to the living voice. Even if this fond dream were realized, it would be a one-sided communication, for we could not catechize the voices of the past. Our Irish historians improved upon this idea: they brought the saints who were their warrants for history into a personal relation with those who had figured in past events, and fabled that their accounts were authenticated by the actual testimony of eye-witnesses and participants of the great deeds of the past. They imagined two means by which this very desirable consummation might be achieved. Either the informant might be recalled from the dead, or by God's grace his life might be miraculously prolonged until the time of the saints and the coming of the written record. For the first method they had the authority of the great Pope Gregory, who had sent forth the English mission and whose fame in Ireland, where he was known as Gregory Goldenmouth, was no less widespread than in England. It was fabled of St. Gregory that, passing through the forum of Trajan one day, he marvelled at its construction, which seemed rather worthy of a Christian than a pagan. For on the arch of Trajan was represented a scene in which Trajan going to the war was asked to do justice to a widow, but bade her wait till his return. 'But,' she answered, 'Lord Trajan, if thou come not back who will help me?' So he did her justice. So Gregory, passing into St. Peter's, offered for Trajan's soul his wonted floods of tears, until by his deserts he obtained the salvation of the emperor's soul.

This story is found in many forms throughout the Middle Ages, appearing in the philosophy of Aquinas, the poetry of Dante and of Piers Plowman, and the art of Roger van der Weyden. But its first appearance is in the life of Gregory by a monk of Whitby written about 713. In an early commentary on Dante by Jacopo della Lana it appears in a different form. There workmen discovered a skull with the tongue still intact. The marvel was told to Gregory and he came to where the head was and bade it speak. The skull answered: 'I am Trajan, emperor of Rome, who held lordship at such and such a time after Christ came down into the Virgin's womb, and I am in Hell because I had not faith.' St. Gregory then inquired concerning the emperor and, hearing the tale of his justice to the widow, brought him to life again by his prayers and baptized him. This theme of the answering skull probably came into the tale from the legend of St. Macarius who, coming upon a dry skull in the desert, questioned it concerning the state of those that had fallen asleep in the faith. The theme of the skull is found in Irish in the Glossary of Cormac,[1] a text of the ninth century, and here the motive has passed from the ecclesiastical to the secular tradition. The tale relates the origin of the name of Corrievreckan, the whirlpool between Ireland and Rathlin Island. It runs thus:

Brecan, books relate, was wont to go carrying merchandise on fifty boats between Ireland and Scotland and they were all drowned at one time in the whirlpool so that not so much as one escaped to tell the tale of destruction. And the way of their death was never known until the blind poet Lugaid came to

[1] *Anecdota*, iv. 27, § 323.

Bangor. His people went upon the strand of Inver Beg and found there a bare and speckled skull and brought it with them to Lugaid. They asked him whose it was and he said to them: 'This is the skull of Brecan's pet dog and it is a little thing remaining of greatness,' said he, 'for Brecan and all his people have been drowned in yonder whirlpool.'

That this combination of themes was known in Ireland in the seventh century is proved by an episode in Tírechán's life of St. Patrick, written at the end of that century.[1] There it is told how Patrick came to a place

where was a sepulchre of marvellous greatness and huge length, and those that were with him marked that it was 120 feet in length, and Patrick said: 'If ye will ye shall see him.' And they said: 'We do so desire.' And he smote the stone at its head with his staff and signed the sepulchre with the sign of the cross and said: 'Open, O Lord, the sepulchre.' And the holy man made the earth to open and there came forth a great voice saying: 'Blessing on thee, holy man, for that thou hast raised me, if for but one hour, from great pain.' Thus saying he wept most bitterly and said: 'I will go with you.' And they said: 'It cannot be that thou shouldest go with us, for men may not abide to see thy face for the fear of thee, but believe in the God of Heaven and accept the baptism of the Lord and thou shalt not return to the place where thou wert, and make known to us of what kin thou art.' And he said: 'I am son's son of Cass son of Glass, and the warband of Mac Con slew me in the reign of Cairbre Nia Fer a hundred years from this day.' And he was baptized and made his confession to God and fell silent and so was laid again in the sepulchre.

It is but a step from this to the tale of the Spectral Chariot of Cú Chulainn in which St. Patrick summons the great hero of the Ulster Saga from the dead to testify of his doings to King Laegaire, plunging through the mist in his chariot drawn by his two famous horses and driven by his charioteer

[1] Stokes, *Vita Tripartita*, ii. 325.

Laeg mac Riangabra.[1] And in the tale of the Finding of the Táin the function of evocation has passed to a poet as in the legend of Corrievreckan. There the poet sits down by the grave of Fergus mac Róig, who had played so great a part in the story.

'He sang an invocation to the stone as though he spake to Fergus himself,' says the tale. 'And at that a great mist fell all about him so that his people might not see him for the space of three days and nights. And Fergus came to him in seemly array, a cloak of green, a hooded tunic with a crimson border, a goldhilted sword, and shoes of bronze, with chestnut hair falling all about him. Fergus related then the whole Táin even as it befell from the beginning unto the end.'[2]

We have passed here very far from the forum of Trajan and the great Pope Gregory into the wild and pagan world of heroic story. But the use of the theme is plain, to authenticate the uncertain record of past things by the clear testimony of contemporaries called up from death to bear their witness. This was the method used for heroic saga. For historic tradition, the saga of the kings, another means was found. We have seen Mongán covering the poets with ridicule by beating them at their own game. And of Mongán it is recorded that he was identical with Finn mac Cumaill, the famous protagonist of the Ossianic saga.[3] It was also told of him that he passed through many shapes of animals and birds, a motive adapted from the theme known to folklorists as the theme of the Oldest Animals. And there gathered about him many strange legends drawn from the inexhaustible treasury of Irish folk-lore. It has indeed been suggested that he is another person of the same name, the historical Ulster princeling having taken over legends which really belonged to an earlier mythical

---

[1] Zimmer, *Z. f. d. Alterthum*, xxxii. 249; Thurneysen, *Heldensage*, 567.
[2] Windisch, *Táin Bó Cualnge*, liii; Thurneysen, *Heldensage*, 252.
[3] Meyer, *Voyage of Bran*, i. 45 ff.

Mongán. I am not now concerned to decide whether this speculation has any basis in fact. The immediate question here is why these legends gathered round a particular historical personage living in a particular place at a particular time. An Irish rationalist of the twelfth century was puzzled by this same question and gave the answer which I should be inclined to give.[1]

'Albeit,' he says, 'certain dealers in antiquarian fable do propound Mongán to have been son of Manannán and wont to enter at his pleasure into divers shapes, yet this we may not credit, rather choosing to take him for one that was but a man of surpassing knowledge and gifted with an intelligence clear and subtle and keen.'

This is indeed the impression which the tales about him, stripped of their fabulous elements, make upon us. He is a typical figure of his type, a scholar-prince interested in the antiquities of his people and meeting and defeating the poets upon their own ground. In the succeeding generation there was to be such another. Mongán died in 624. In 636 was fought the battle of Moira,[2] one of the most famous battles of the North round which many traditions clustered. In the battle Cenn Faelad, son of Ailill, son of Baetán, a near descendant of two high kings of Ireland, was wounded in the head and, says the legend, his brain of forgetting was stricken out of him. He was carried for healing to Toomregan to the house of the abbot Briccíne

where the three streets meet between the houses of the three professors. And there were three schools in the place, a school of Latin learning, a school of Irish law and a school of Irish poetry. And everything that he would hear of the recitations of the three schools every day he would have it by heart every night. And he fitted a pattern of poetry to these matters and

[1] O'Grady, *Silva Gadelica*, i. 391.
[2] O'Donovan, *Cath Muighe Rath*.

wrote them on slates and tablets and set them in a vellum book.

It has been argued by Professor Mac Neill[1] that here we have the beginning of the written tradition of certain types of vernacular matter, and we find in later manuscripts a number of texts, legal and grammatical, attributed to Cenn Faelad. How far these are really his may be a matter of controversy, but there can be little doubt that writings by him existed in the period when the vernacular learning was being eagerly cultivated. He is the first poet quoted in the Annals, and the historical verses attributed to him all relate to his own kindred of the Northern Uí Neill. He is given the title *sapiens* in the texts, a technical term meaning a head teacher or professor in the monastic schools. It is in this period that the Annals begin to record the deaths of *sapientes*. Before 700 the Annals of Ulster record the deaths of Cummíne Fota of Clonfert whose teacher was the Colmán Moccu Chluasaig to whom one of the earliest of Irish hymns is attributed (d. 662), of Sarán Ua Critáin of Tisaran in King's County (d. 662), of Ailerán of Clonard, County Meath (d. 665), and of Lochéne abbot of Kildare (d. 696), to all of whom this title is given. All of these, and no doubt many others unrecorded, must have been active about the middle of the seventh century, the period of Cenn Faelad. And Bede in a famous passage tells us that at this very time English students were crossing to Ireland in great numbers in quest of learning.

At that time there were many of the English nation, both of noble and of lesser rank, who, whether for divine study or to lead a more continent life, had left their native land and had withdrawn to Ireland. Certain among them gave themselves up willingly to the monastic way of life, while others rather went about from cell to cell of the teachers and took pleasure in cultivating study. And all these the Irish most freely

[1] *Early Irish Laws and Institutions*, 84 ff.

received, and made it their study to provide them with food from day to day without any charge, with books to read and with free teaching.[1]

It would be an easy matter to illustrate this passage with striking examples, but perhaps the most typical and the most famous case is that of Aldfrid son of Osuiu, who became king of Northumbria in 671. Bede says of him, in words which recall the passage just quoted:

Shortly before this he cultivated study among the Irish, submitting to a voluntary exile for the love of learning.

Alcuin also writes thus of him:

From youth's first years in sacred learning dipped / Powerful in discourse, philosopher / Keenwitted, king and master in the schools.

We know from Bede that Aldfrid studied in Iona with Adamnan, and it may be taken as more than probable that the Irish tradition of his activities in Ireland has a basis in fact. It would be difficult on any other hypothesis to explain why he is so constantly reckoned as one of the great Irish sages. He had a special name in Ireland, Fland Fína, Fland the son of Fína. It does not appear to have been observed before that this Fína was the cousin of the great scholar Cenn Faelad. This may well explain Aldfrid's visit to Ireland and his lasting reputation there. Cenn Faelad died in 678, Aldfrid's father Osuiu in 671, and Aldfrid himself in 705. He may well have been in Ireland about 671–6, the period at which Bede says that Englishmen of noble birth were frequenting the Irish schools. In Irish manuscripts of a later date we find various texts attributed to Aldfrid:[2] a poem in which he is represented as travelling throughout Ireland and praising the people he met there, and certain collections of a proverbial type such as are commonly attributed to the wise men of old. None of these

[1] *Hist. Eccl.* iii. xxvii.   [2] *Speculum,* iv. 95 ff.

can be of his composition, but they prove the existence of a tradition that he had learnt Irish and that, as a devoted scholar of his uncle Cenn Faelad, he had like him composed in that language. And the fact that Bede attributes his great learning to his studies in Ireland is a sufficient proof of the estimation in which the scholarship of that country was held in Northumbria.

The tradition of Cenn Faelad and his nephew Aldfrid justifies us in assuming that the vernacular was actively cultivated for literary purposes in Ireland about the middle of the seventh century. And we have seen that the tale of Mongán mac Fiachna suggests that at the beginning of that century the princes and the poets and clerics of south-eastern Ulster were vying in the study of their country's antiquities. There is much other evidence to support this conclusion. And the evidence points to the great monastery of Bangor on the shores of Belfast Lough as the centre of historical studies at that time. The monastery of Bangor was founded in 555. The founder was St. Comgall, who came from the Pictish territory of Dalaradia and was always regarded as the patron saint of that district, although his monastery was in Ulidian territory. A few miles from Bangor there was another famous monastery, Movilla, founded about 540 by St. Finnian. Both of these monasteries were great centres of scholarship, and many of the saints and scholars of Ireland in the sixth century were educated in one or other of them. The great missionary saint, Columba, studied under St. Finnian at Movilla, and St. Comgall of Bangor co-operated with him in his work among the Picts of Scotland, probably acting as interpreter. It is clear that particular attention was paid to historical studies at Bangor, and the earliest Irish chronicle was probably a production of that house. It has been attributed with good reason to Sinlán Moccu Mín, that Sinlanus who is described in the list of abbots in the Antiphonary of

Bangor as the 'famed teacher of the world' (*famosus mundi magister*). A note in the eighth-century Würzburg codex[1] shows that Sinlán studied that art of ecclesiastical computation which was so closely allied with history in those days. It runs:

> Mosinu Maccu Mín, scribe and abbot of Bangor, was the first of the Irish who learned the Computus by rote from a certain Greek. Afterwards Mocuaróc Maccu Neth Semon whom the Romans styled doctor of the whole world, a pupil of the aforesaid scribe in the island called Crannach of Downpatrick, committed this knowledge to writing lest it should lapse from memory.

This would suggest that Sinlán was the teacher in the monastic school of Bangor on Cranny Island in Strangford Lough, and it is possible that the chronicle, like the Computus, was compiled under his supervision rather than actually written by his own hand.

Besides the Annals, which consist of concise and rather jejune notices of events, there developed in Ireland a form of narrative history, the evolution of which by a process of accretion may be traced from the seventh to the twelfth century. This is the chronicle known as the Book of Conquest or Occupation (*Lebor Gabála*), which served as a kind of introduction to the historic sagas which recorded the exploits of the kings. For this prehistory of Ireland, recording in detail the successive invasions of Ireland in a period which stretched from before the Flood down to the borders of historic time, it was necessary to provide a living witness. It would have been necessary to summon up whole hosts from the dead, if, as with the heroic saga, the testimony of eye-witnesses was required to substantiate every decisive event in the long process of centuries. Here again a prince of one of the dynasties of the North was chosen to bear witness. This was Tuan son of Cairell, the king of Ulster who

[1] *Thesaurus Palaeohibernicus*, ii. 285.

died in 581 or 587. It was fabled of Tuan that he, too, like Mongán, passed through many shapes, taking the form of one animal after another and witnessing as a contemporary all the invasions of Ireland till at last he was born a man, the son of Cairell.[1] When St. Finnian of Movilla came to Ulster with his gospel, that is, the famous copy of the Vulgate New Testament which he was the first to introduce into Ireland, there came to meet him a venerable cleric who bade him welcome and asked the saint and his company to go with him, and they performed the duties of the Lord's day. Thereupon Finnian asked him to tell them his name. Said he to them:

Of the men of Ulster am I. I am Tuan son of Cairell son of Muiredach Red-neck. I have taken this hermitage in which thou art upon my father's hereditary lands. Tuan son of Starn son of Partholón's brother, that was my name of old at the first.

He then related to them all his transformations and told of all the companies of men he had seen in the occupation of Ireland.

In another part of Ireland a similar story is told of one Fintan mac Bóchra who seems rather to represent the tradition of the South and of Clonmacnois.[2] Fintan is also represented as a shape-shifter, and in one version of the Book of Conquest the two traditions are reconciled by the statement that Tuan and Fintan were identical. These tales betray the same impulse to authenticate real or invented history by living, contemporary witness which we have seen at work in the domain of heroic saga. And the connexion of Tuan with Finnian of Movilla proves that the historical movement was in active prosecution in that region of Ulster where we have seen the annalistic record beginning.

[1] Meyer, *Voyage of Bran*, ii. 285 ff.   [2] *Anecdota*, i. 24–39.

I may perhaps go one step farther and claim for Bangor
one of the earliest, the most famous, and the most beautiful
of Irish poems. No Irish cycle of story came home so intimately to medieval Europe as that of the oversea voyages
represented by the Navigation of St. Brendan. But Brendan
was only one among many who set out into the shoreless
sea to seek the land of promise beyond the sunset. And of
all their stories none is older, none lovelier than the Voyage
of Bran.[1] This tale as it has come down to us consists in the
main of two poems, in one of which a fairy woman lures
Bran oversea by picturing the delights of the Elysian island
lost in the sea, while in the other the sea-god Manannán son
of Ler prophesies of Mongán who was to be begotten by
him in a later age. Manannán is the divinity of that sea
which washes the coasts of Ulster on the East and Mongán
a prince of Dalaradia, the Pictish kingdom which had
Comgall of Bangor, the chief saint of that race, for its patron
and protector. A curious tale of the twelfth century[2] tells
of the wars between Fiachna, Mongán's father, and another
Fiachna, son of Demmán, king of that territory of Ulster in
which the monastery of Bangor was founded. The Pictish
Fiachna was constantly victorious in battle over the Ulidian
Fiachna, and the defeated king reproached Comgall for
permitting the lord of his district to be overcome in war.
'For which of us do you pray to your God?' he asked. 'I
pray for both of you,' answered the diplomatic saint. 'But
for which do you pray most earnestly?' 'For the lord of the
land in which I was born.' In the conflict of loyalties Comgall stood by his own race. And when in 824 the Danes
ravaged Bangor, it was to the monastery of Antrim hard
by Moylinny, the strong place of the kings of his people,
that his relics were carried to rest among his own kin. It is
natural to conclude that the tale of Mongán, so intimately
linked with the tradition of Dalaradia, was shaped in

[1] Meyer, *Voyage of Bran*, i. 1 ff.   [2] O'Grady, *Silva Gadelica*, ii. 427.

Bangor, the chief monastery of that kingdom, though established upon an alien soil.

Bran's voyage started from Lough Foyle. And it will not be amiss to quote a beautiful story from the Latin life of Comgall, which links the name of that saint to that great arm of the sea.[1]

'The blessed abbot Comgall,' says the tale, 'saw by the brink of Lough Foyle swans swimming upon the lake and most sweetly singing. Then the brethren besought the elder that in place of the consolation of food he would summon the swans to them that they might stroke them with their hands. For it was the time when the brethren should eat, but their food was not prepared for them. The good father says to them: "If such is God's will, be it so done." And as he spoke, the swans, constrained by God's command, took wing towards the servants of Christ and one of them stayed in his flight in the bosom of the holy elder Comgall. And thereafter, when he gave them leave, they resorted again to the lake.'

It is perhaps not fanciful to see in this passage of prose something of that poetry so exquisitely distilled in the verses of the Voyage of Bran and to feel some prophecy of that later story, The Fate of the Children of Ler, in which the offspring of the sea-god, magically transmuted into swans, are shown floating disconsolately on the waters of the Foyle.

The poetry of the North, as represented in the verses of Cenn Faelad and the Voyage of Bran, is all composed in quatrains of numbered syllables with regular rhyme and a moderate use of alliteration. In the South a more archaic form was practised. This is the old rhetorical verse with an irregular number of syllables to the line, governed by accent and using chain alliteration. Here a number of words alliterate on the same consonant or vowel, then a fresh alliteration succeeds and so on to the end of the poem.

[1] Plummer, *VSH.* ii. 16.

Kuno Meyer illustrates this form of verse in his essays on the oldest Irish poetry, taking his examples from the genealogies.[1] It is to be noted that this form of poetry appears regularly in the genealogies of Leinster and Munster, and there can be little doubt that it was chiefly practised in the south. One practitioner of this style was particularly famous, and his poetry has come down to us in a form which suggests that it was written down at an early date.

When St. Brendan of Clonfert was journeying in Munster he met by the way a certain layman named Colmán mac Léníne. And he said to him: Repent, for God summons thee to salvation and thou shalt be as a faultless dove in God's presence. This was that Colmán mac Léníne who was excelling among the saints for his life and learning. For it was he that founded the church of Cloyne, which is today a cathedral church and famous in Munster.[2]

Colmán had been a poet in his unregenerate days and some of his poetry of that time has come down to us. This has all been printed by Rudolf Thurneysen who claims that it has descended from the first in a written tradition.[3] As Colmán belongs to the second half of the sixth century, this would suggest that the writing down of the vernacular had already begun in Munster by the year 600, the period when we have seen the monks of Bangor in the North active in the compilation of historical material and the collection of the vernacular traditions. The primary business of a poet, it is constantly emphasized in our texts, was the composition of eulogies and satires, and Colmán's poems are mostly of this kind. One instance may be given, composed, it is plain, in the days before his conversion and addressed

[1] *Über die älteste irische Dichtung*, i and ii (Berlin, Prussian Academy, 1913, 1914).

[2] Plummer, *VSH*. i. 102.

[3] *ZCP*. xix. 193 ff.

to a Munster king. One stanza only survives in which the poet speaks of his sword:

> As clowns to kings, as pennies to a pound,
> As kitchen wenches to princesses crowned,
> As kings to thee, to sweet songs catches roared,
> As dips to candles all swords to my sword.

Colmán remained in Munster tradition as the type of a poet, and is affectionately quoted by Cormac mac Cuilennáin, king-bishop of Cashel, himself both cleric and poet, in his glossary; and in a later age the O'Dalys, the chief poetic family of medieval Ireland, claimed that Dálach, their ancestor, had studied under him and had learnt from him the art which became hereditary in his family.

All the literature with which we have been dealing is devoted to the praise of Ireland and of its noble families. It is animated throughout by an intense love of the very soil of Ireland, of its high places and the traditions which had accumulated around them. And yet by a strange paradox the Irish are the first of the missionary peoples of Europe, famous everywhere in the early Middle Ages for their *consuetudo peregrinandi*, that passion for exile in foreign lands which had such momentous results for European civilization. The paradox is easy to resolve. It has often been observed that in Ireland there were no martyrs for the faith. And in a homily of the seventh century there is a threefold classification of martyrdom in an ascending scale.[1]

Now this is white martyrdom for a man, when for God's sake he parts from everything that he loves, though he suffers fasting and labour thereby. And green martyrdom is when he endures labour in penitence and repentance. And red martyrdom is the submission to the cross and tribulation for Christ's sake.

The great missionaries went into exile as into martyrdom, giving up all that they loved most dearly. The Middle-

---

[1] *Thesaurus*, ii. 247.

Irish life of St. Columcille sets out their doctrine in detail.
It opens with a text from Genesis giving God's command
to Abraham to leave his fatherland to seek the land of
promise:[1]

Leave thy country and thy land and thy neighbour in the
flesh and thine own fatherland for my sake and get thee into
the country that I will show thee.

Now the good action which God enjoined upon the father
of the faithful, that is, on Abraham, is a duty for his sons after
him, that is, on all the faithful, to fulfil: to leave their soil and
their land, their wealth and their worldly joy for the sake of
the Lord of the elements and to go into perfect exile in imita-
tion of him.

Now there are three ways in which a man leaves his fatherland when he goes on pilgrimage, and in one of these ways he
receives no reward from God and in two of them he does
receive reward. For when a man leaves his fatherland in the
body alone and his mind is not separated from his sins and
vices and desires not to perform virtue and right action, in such
pilgrimage there accrues no fruit or profit to the soul, but
labour and a vain corporal travail, for little profit is it to a man
to leave his fatherland if he do not good away from it. For as
regards Abraham himself it was after he had left his dear
country and sundered himself from it bodily that God gave
that counsel to him, saying: Leave thy country. Think no
more of thy soil and thy land and let it not be in thy mind to
return thither again. As though it were this that God would
say clearly to Abraham: From this time forth in thy pilgrimage
shun in body and soul the sins and vices of the land wherein
thou hast dwelt till now in the body, for it is all one to a man
as though he still dwelt in his fatherland if he mimic in his
pilgrimage the ways of his fatherland, for it is not by journeying
or by the straying of the body that one draws near to God, but
by the performance of good and virtuous actions. In another
way a man leaves his fatherland in fervour of heart and in soul,
though he leave it not in body, as befalls men in orders to spend

[1] Stokes, *Lives of Saints from the Book of Lismore*, 20.

their lives in their countries until they die, for the service of churches and of the lay folk detains them in the lands in which they are, for the great profit they do them; since it is for no carnal cause that they abide in their fatherland, their fervent purpose is counted as pilgrimage for them with the Lord. And in another way a man leaves his fatherland wholly in body and soul, as the twelve apostles left it and the folk of perfect pilgrimage to whom the Lord foretold great good, saying in the Gospel: 'Take heed of this, for from a few to a multitude ye have forsaken for my sake your country and your carnal kindred, your wealth and your worldly happiness that ye may receive a hundredfold of good from Me here in the world and life everlasting yonder after the sentence of doom.' These in sooth are they of the perfect pilgrimage, in whose person the prophet speaks: 'I give thee thanks for it, O God; I have pilgrimage and exile in the world even as the elders who went before.'

It was from the very district with which we have been dealing, Bangor and its neighbourhood, where the local and national traditions were so eagerly cultivated, that the great missions started. St. Columcille studied at Movilla and St. Comgall assisted him in his conversion of the Picts of Scotland. St. Columbanus went out from Bangor, and a direct consequence of his labours was the foundation of Luxeuil and St. Gall and Bobbio, the chief centres of religion and scholarship in a Europe struggling out of the Dark Ages. And we may find an evidence from Bangor tradition that the complete abnegation demanded by the Irish doctrine of pilgrimage was a hard saying to these lovers of their fatherland. It was not necessary to leave Ireland to go on a pilgrimage. A marked feature of the lives of the saints is what at first sight appears to be a constant restlessness. They never abide in one stay, but leave their own district and wander all Ireland over, founding monasteries as they go. It is rare to find the chief foundation of an Irish saint in his own country-side. And when laymen entered religion, they left their own district and their friends and joined a community at a distance as the doctrine of pilgrimage demanded. A tale in the life of Comgall shows us one of those Irish kings who gave up their earthly rule and submitted themselves to the harsh discipline of a distant religious house.[1]

Cormac son of Diarmuid, a king of Leinster, offered himself with three strong places in Leinster to God and St. Comgall. And he came to the province of Ulster and became a monk with St. Comgall in his monastery of Bangor. Thereafter the ancient enemy inspired in his heart a great and sore longing for his fatherland and his children, his kindred and his dear friends. And he, much troubled in mind, came to the holy father Comgall and confessed to him that he could not endure longer there if he might not visit and behold his fatherland. Now the holy father Comgall, discerning that he could not detain him there, dismissed him and certain of the brethren with him. They set forth on the journey and straightway, his holy abbot praying on his behalf, there fell upon him a slumber sent from God on a hill that looked over Bangor, and he slept there from the first hour of the day until nones and dreamed this dream. For it seemed to him that he made a circuit of all the bounds of Leinster and walked among its beautiful monasteries and strong places, and went all about its flowering plains and winsome meads, and ruled in his own kingdom, and his princes and lords and chief men and all other the glories of his kingdom were seated around him. And when he was fulfilled of all these things, he awaked in great weariness at the hour of nones. And he conceived a hatred of all he had seen by God's aid, and of his own will he turned back to his holy abbot Comgall and told him all these things. And he abode there in the life of religion until his death.

To many another Irishman, as he went the long roads of Europe in those days of the great mission, some such visions, perhaps not always so readily dispelled, must often

---

[1] Plummer, *VSH.* ii. 16.

have come, for it is not given to all men to find complete oblivion and the perfect pilgrimage. And maybe, as they thus yielded to the irresistible weakness of the flesh, some long-forgotten strain of poetry sounded in their ears and, walking in recollection among the monasteries and high places and flowering plains and winsome meads, they pondered the lore of the *dindshenchas* and went once more for a fleeting moment in the ways of the lost country of their home.

II

EXILES AND HERMITS

IT was in the ninth century that some wandering scholar from Leinster kept a commonplace book upon the shores of Lake Constance. He must have written down whatever in his day's reading took his fancy—notes from a commentary on the *Aeneid*, excerpts from the fathers, some church hymns, a brief glossary of Greek words, some Greek declensions (not very accurate), and some very peculiar natural history.[1] Amid a huddle of other sayings he has written down, too, that proverb of exile—'caelum non animum mutant qui trans mare currunt'—which the young Milton was afterwards to adapt to the album of a Neapolitan refugee at Geneva. Milton added a verse of his own stern poetry:

> If virtue feeble were
> Heaven itself would stoop to her.

And so our Irish wanderer remembered the poetry of his native land, perhaps his own poetry, and set down casually beside his Latin commonplaces and Greek declensions those verses which were to make him immortal. It is the first example we have in manuscript of the personal poetry of the Irish, and it is very characteristic that the verses should be concerned with the antics of a scholar's cat. One is reminded of the quaint cat that twists its elongated form round the litany on the first page of the contemporary Irish Stowe Missal. This is the poem in which the student tells us of this companion.[2]

> I and Pangur Bán my cat,
> 'Tis a like task we are at:
> Hunting mice is his delight,
> Hunting words I sit all night.

[1] *Thesaurus*, ii. xxxii.　　　　[2] *Thesaurus*, ii. 293.

Better far than praise of men
'Tis to sit with book and pen;
Pangur bears me no ill will,
He too plies his simple skill.

'Tis a merry thing to see
At our tasks how glad are we,
When at home we sit and find
Entertainment to our mind.

Oftentimes a mouse will stray
In the hero Pangur's way;
Oftentimes my keen thought set
Takes a meaning in its net.

'Gainst the wall he sets his eye
Full and fierce and sharp and sly;
'Gainst the wall of knowledge I
All my little wisdom try.

When a mouse darts from its den
O how glad is Pangur then!
O what gladness do I prove
When I solve the doubts I love!

So in peace our tasks we ply,
Pangur Bán, my cat, and I;
In our arts we find our bliss,
I have mine and he has his.

Practice every day has made
Pangur perfect in his trade;
I get wisdom day and night
Turning darkness into light.

It is to be hoped that white Pangur remained faithful to
his master and did not yield to that peregrinatory passion
(*consuetudo peregrinandi*) which we know to be characteristic
of cats, and which Walafrid Strabo notes as a chief mark of
the Irish of the ninth century. A later poet tells us that
Irish cats were not free of this defect. Above the complaint

'The white cat has gone straying from me' he sets this
cynical comment on feline and human nature:[1]

> The kitling cat
> Whose nurturing thou labourest at,
> When he is come to cat's estate
> Goes wild and flees thee soon or late.
>
> 'Tis so with evil natures still
> For, give them, as they grow, their will,
> And, when to man's estate they're come,
> They'll fly their father and their home.

I cannot resist the temptation to add here a little tale of a
cat's pilgrimage from the Book of Leinster.[2]

Three students there were of the men of Ireland that went
on pilgrimage. With zeal and heart's love they went that
journey. Three loaves was all the provender they took to sea.
'I'll take the kitling with me,' said one of them. When they
were come to the shoulder of the sea, 'In Christ's name,' said
they, 'let us cast our oars into the sea and give ourselves into
God's hands.' And so they did. It was not long till with
Christ's help they came to an island. 'It is a lovely isle,' said
they, 'with water and a plenty of firewood in it. So let us make
a church upon the island.' And so they did. Their cat goes
and drags to them goodly salmon, as much as three salmons
every day. 'This pilgrimage of ours is no pilgrimage at all
now,' said they, 'for we have brought our provisions with us,
that is, our cat to be our provider. We will eat no more of
the cat's food.' So they abode six days without food till there
came a provision from Christ upon the altar, half a wheaten
loaf and a piece of fish for each one of them.

The sequel of the tale in the Book of Leinster tells us how
the human pilgrims died one after the other until only one
grey old man was left to carry the burden of prayer and

[1] *Gaelic Journal*, vii. 116.

[2] *Mélusine*, iv, cols. 6–11, cf. Stokes, *Lives of the Saints from the Book of
Lismore*, p. viii.

praise originally borne by the three. The poor cat had a gloomier fate. For, living on the salmon which its masters rejected, it swelled to the proportions of a monster and was destroyed by St. Brendan when, on his voyagings, he came to bring release of death to the last survivor of that pious company.

But it is time to return from the cat to his master, the wandering Leinsterman in Europe. The character of the poetry which he has interspersed amid the evidences of his variegated learning indicates clearly enough the district of his origin. First there is a bardic poem in eulogy of a chief of north Leinster, Aed son of Diarmait son of Muiredach. This is among our earliest examples of the panegyrical poetry so inordinately developed by the later bards. And as I do not propose to exemplify further this part of Irish poetry, a translation may be attempted.[1]

> Kindler of glory's embers,
> Aed, goodly hand of giving;
> Comeliest that song remembers
> By pastoral Roeriu living.
>
> A mighty shaft and loyal
> Whom glory overarches;
> Of all men else most royal
> In grassy Maistiu's marches.
>
> My love—if such his pleasure—
> To Dermot's son I bring it;
> My song—more worth than treasure—
> To his high praise I sing it.
>
> Dear name! renowned in story,
> Aed! no man may decry him;
> Where Liffey flows in glory
> Fame's voice shall ne'er bely him.

[1] *Thesaurus*, ii. 295.

Grandchild of that fierce fighter
Muireach, a cliff of splendours,
Honour—no fame is brighter—
To his race Cualu renders.

A stately tree, a glowing
Jewel whom strife embolden;
A silver sapling growing
From soil of princes olden.

Songs at the alefeast ringing,
Scales climbed of comely measures,
Bards with their heady singing
Acclaim Aed and his pleasures.

In this poem—perhaps of the eighth century—the Irish panegyric style which was to rule for near ten centuries is already formed. We have materials for tracing its evolution from the sixth century onwards,[1] and its characteristics are at all periods substantially the same. The style is always strict and concise; using metaphor in preference to simile; indulging in asyntactical constructions for which the exclamatory character of Irish sentence structure gives ample excuse; bold and barbaric in its terms and figures; and tending always to treat the chieftain eulogized as an abstract compendium of princely qualities rather than as a being subject to the ebb and flow of the more ordinary impulses.

The earliest examples of this poetry that we have are eulogies of the Milesian dynasties of Leinster and Munster. The placenames in the poem from the St. Paul manuscript point to north Leinster as the district of its composition. And much of the material that we have for the early non-official poetry points to this same Leinster–Munster district as the most productive region in the time of the saints. Poetry, indeed, was only one growth in a field of intense intellectual and religious activity. Most of the Latin manu-

[1] Meyer, *Über die älteste irische Dichtung.*

scripts that have come down to us from the old Irish Church were written within the limits of the district. The chief theological literature, Latin or Irish, arose in the country lying south of a line drawn from Clonmacnoise through Clonard to Tallaght near Dublin. The main centres outside of this region, Bangor in the Ards of Ulster, and Iona off the Scottish coast, were in close and constant communion with the South. Comgall, the founder of Bangor, is said to have studied under Fintan of Clonenagh in Leix; whether this is true in fact or not is of little importance to the argument, for in any case it denotes that there was a close connexion between Bangor and Clonenagh. Columcille's relations with Bangor and the South are very marked, and there was a regular intercommunication between Iona and these districts. In fact, if we study the lives of the saints of the sixth and seventh centuries we find that Columcille is to these writers the typical Irish saint far more than Patrick, who in these records is a somewhat intermittent and shadowy figure. The early disciplinary and canonical literature which one would have expected to find issuing from the metropolitan centre is to a considerable extent of southern origin. The writers of penitentials were Finnian of Clonard and Cuimíne Fota, a markedly Munster writer. There is some reason for believing that the collection of Irish canons was first put together in the present County Cork, and Sir George Warner has proved that the Stowe Missal was written at Tallaght in the ninth century.

The *Félire* of Oengus, with its commentary, is particularly illuminating in this connexion. There seems no reason for questioning the accuracy of the tradition that this festology was composed at the beginning of the ninth century by Oengus Céile Dé and at Tallaght. The tradition further states that the work was begun at Cúil Bennachair near Terryglass in Lower Ormond, continued at Clonenagh, and concluded at Tallaght. There would be nothing surprising in this; for there is evidence of an intimate religious and literary connexion between Terryglass and Clonenagh, which were under one abbot, and Tallaght. Thus Maeldíthruib, the anchorite of Terryglass, is mentioned as in unity with Maelruain in the Book of Leinster (fcs. 370 c 48), and in other documents the two are brought into connexion. Also it is plain that much of the material for the history of the Irish Church collected in the Book of Leinster (which was written in great part at Terryglass) is drawn from the collections of Tallaght. It is significant in this connexion that much of the material used in the commentary of the *Félire* occurs also in the Book of Leinster. And if we compare the texts and collections bearing on church history in the Book of Leinster with the commentary on the *Félire*, we are immediately struck by the fact that the same saints and the same episodes are brought into relief in both. The saints to whom the commentary gives most space are Columcille, Bridget, Ciarán of Saigir, Moling, Ita of Killeedy and other Leinster and Munster saints. Only a few lines are devoted to Patrick in the comment on his day. This commentary, then, shows us the traditions current regarding the saints of Leinster and Munster in the period from the ninth to the twelfth century. One may show how aptly these various authorities supplement one another, by citing a tale and poem dealing with Moling, two verses of which occur in our St. Paul manuscript, while the complete text is found in the Book of Leinster and in the commentary on the *Félire*. In these two last sources, the poem is prefaced by a prose tale clearly of later origin, but so delightful in its quaint theology that it must not be omitted:[1]

Once upon a time Moling was at prayers in his church, and he saw a lad coming towards him, a goodly lad arrayed in purple raiment.

'Hail, cleric!' says he.

[1] Stokes, *Félire*, 154 ff. (Henry Bradshaw Society, 1905).

'The same to thee,' says Moling.

'Why greetest thou not me with a blessing?' says the lad.

'Who art thou?'

'I am Christ, son of God.'

'I know not that,' says Moling. 'When Christ would come to have speech with the Culdees, 'twas not in purple raiment or in kingly guise that he would come, but after the fashion of hapless men, as a leper or a man diseased.'

'Is it doubt of me thou hast?' says the lad. 'Who thinkest thou, then, that I am?'

'Methinks,' says Moling, 'thou art the devil come to do me injury.'

'Ill for thee that unfaith,' says the lad.

'Well,' says Moling, 'here is thy witness after thee, Christ's gospels.' And he lifted up the gospel.

'Lift it not, cleric,' says he. 'Perchance I am he thou thinkest. I am, indeed, the man of tribulation.'

'What brought thee hither?' says Moling.

'To get thy blessing.'

'I will not give it,' says Moling. 'Thou dost not merit it. And it would avail thee little,' says Moling.

Then says the devil: 'If thou shouldest bathe thee in a honey vat, thyself and thy raiment, then would the honey scent cleave to thee, didst thou not wash thy raiment.'

'What intendest thou by that?' says Moling.

'This I intend,' says the devil. 'Though thy blessing profit me nothing, yet were its promise, its favour and its bloom about me.'

'That shall not be,' says Moling, 'for thou hast not merited it.'

'Well,' says he. 'Vent a full curse on me then.'

'What good were that to thee?' says Moling.

'Easy to answer, O cleric! The curse will leave its venom and its hurt on thy lips in passing over them.'

'Hence with thee!' says Moling. 'Thou meritest not a blessing.'

'Better were it for me, could I merit it,' says he. 'How shall I earn it?'

'By serving God,' says Moling.

'Alack!' says he, 'I cannot do it.'

'Study then.'

'Neither can I study and it avails me not.'

'Fast then.'

'I have been fasting since the world began and I am no whit the better of it.'

'Then bow the knee in prayer.'

'I cannot crook my knees forward to kneel, for they are turned backwards.'

'Go from me then,' says Moling, 'for I can neither instruct thee nor preserve thee.'

On this the devil said:

> Pure gold, bright sky about the sun,
> A silver goblet filled with wine,
> An angel wise is every one
> That still hath done God's will divine.
>
> A caught bird fluttering in the snare,
> A leaky ship that wild winds shake,
> A wineglass drained, a rotten tree—
> Even such they be that God's law break.
>
> A breathing branch that flowers in spring,
> A vessel brimmed with honey sweet,
> A precious ruby beyond price—
> Such he that follows Christ's own feet.
>
> A hollow nut that none desire,
> A savour foul, a rotten wood,
> A flowerless crabtree growing wild,
> Are those defiled that Christ withstood.
>
> The man that does Christ's heavenly will,
> He is the sun that warms the year,
> God's image through his heart doth pass,
> He is a glass of crystal clear.
>
> A racehorse straining for the goal,
> Heaven is the mark for which he tries;
> That chariot driven by a king,
> A precious thing shall be his prize.

A sun that warms all Heaven round,
God loves him more than things of price;
A noble temple and divine,
A golden shrine of sacrifice.

An altar with the wine outpoured
Where sweet choirs sing in linen stoled;
A chalice with God's blood therein
Of *findruine* or precious gold.

Our manuscript not unreasonably deprives the devil of the authorship of this beautiful and orthodox poem and gives it to Moling himself. Modern scholars have, with some reservations, supported this ascription, but the evidence is not very decisive. If the ascription could be maintained, we should possess a poem by Moling to put beside the Gospel of St. John in the Book of Moling, which was almost certainly written by the saint's own hand.

The last of the poems in the St. Paul manuscript is connected with a protégé of Moling. The battle of Mag Rath fought in 637 was one of the decisive battles of early Irish history. And many traditions accumulated around it. Three results of the battle are particularly acclaimed in the Irish literary tradition. They are these:[1]

Three were the glories of that battle: the defeat of Congal Claen in his falsehood by Domnall in his truth; the madness of Suibne Geilt; and the taking of Cenn Faelad's brain of forgetfulness out of his head. And (adds the commentator) it is not the fact of Suibne's madness that makes a glory of the battle, but the stories and poems he left in Ireland after him.

These stories and poems, as they were recorded by a later generation, are to be found in the text known as the *Buile Šuibne*, so admirably edited for the Irish Texts Society by Mr. O'Keeffe. In that text, as elsewhere, the inspired madman is associated with St. Moling in whose arms he

---

[1] *Ancient Laws*, iii. 88; cf. *Auraicept*, 6.

died. And so it is natural that our wandering scholar,
having written down a poem of Moling's, should add one
by Suibne Geilt. The poem is somewhat obscure, but it
appears to refer to one of those woodland oratories in which
the Irish hermits delighted to dwell:[1]

The Ivy Crest

In Tuaim Inbhir here I find
No great house such as mortals build,
A hermitage that fits my mind
With sun and moon and starlight filled.

'Twas Gobbán shaped it cunningly
—This is a tale that lacks not proof—
And my heart's darling in the sky,
Christ, was the thatcher of its roof.

Over my house rain never falls,
There comes no terror of the spear;
It is a garden without walls
And everlasting light shines here.

We have now read all the Irish poems in our manuscript; and we may sum up what is known of the writer of
it. He was interested, we have seen, in theology, in grammar, and in poetry. He transcribes part of a commentary
on Virgil. He quotes a line of Horace, a line which has
been a comfort to exiles in all ages. He has at least a bow-
ing acquaintance with Greek. He quotes among the fathers
Augustine's *De Civitate Dei* (the favourite reading of Charlemagne) and Jerome's version of the Eusebian *Chronicle*. He
is interested in Latin hymn poetry. And, finally, he trea-
sures the poetry of his native land. We have seen reason to
believe that he came from Leinster. Perhaps it would not
be overventuresome to assert that he came from Kildare.
The poems he quotes, so far as their localities are to be
ascertained, come from County Kildare and County Car-

[1] *Thesaurus*, ii. 294.

low. And it is interesting to note that the three place-names in the poem on Aed—Life, Roeriu, Maistiu—appear in a similar connexion in a ninth-century poem in praise of Bridget of Kildare.[1] Can we give any reason why an Irish scholar from Kildare with just these interests in theology, grammar, and poetry should be wandering in the Carolingian Empire in the first half of the ninth century? I think we can.

In the year 848 the men of Munster and Leinster won a great victory over the Northmen at Sciath Nechtain in Leinster. At this time Charles the Bald was showing great favour to the Irish. He had just (846) confirmed the canon of the Council of Meaux (845) re-establishing the Irish hospices which served as caravanserais for the pilgrims of that country. And the Irish decided to send an embassy to acquaint him with their victory over the universal enemy. A contemporary chronicler, Prudentius of Troyes, has this entry under the year 848: 'The Irish are victorious over the invading Northmen with the help of Christ and drive them from their borders. For which cause the king of the Irish sends an embassy to Charles in token of peace and friendship, bringing gifts and requesting a passage for the king to Rome.'[2]

There is some reason for supposing that the famous scholar Sedulius of Liège came on this embassy. He first appears in Liège in 848 and panegyrical poems by him addressed to Charles the Bald in that year still exist. From 848 to 858 we have evidence of his intense literary activity at Liège, Metz, Cologne, and in the surrounding country. And a number of manuscripts written by him and by members of his immediate circle still exist. These manuscripts are interesting from many points of view—for classical philology, for the history of Greek studies, for the text of

---

[1] Meyer, *Hail Brigit* (Halle, 1912).
[2] Cf. Einhard, *Vita Caroli Magni*, cap. 16.

the Scriptures, for the culture of the Carolingian Empire, and for the valuable Irish glosses they contain. But their interest for our present purpose consists in their marginalia. Irish scribes—and only Irish scribes at that time—had a habit of setting down in the margins and on blank spaces of their manuscripts personal memoranda, invocations of saints, little fragments of verse, and all the flotsam and jetsam of idle fancy. This is a marked characteristic of Irish scribes in all ages. And we owe to it the preservation of most of the personal and informal literature of the Irish. One may imagine that the dull task of transcribing theological and grammatical texts fretted these exuberant minds, and their impatient and erratic fancy overflowed into the margins. They were, perhaps, like that anonymous poet and monk who complains of the difficulty he found in concentrating on the singing of the psalms.[1]

Straying Thought

My thought it is a wanton ranger,
It skips away;
I fear 'twill bring my soul in danger
On Judgement Day.

For when the holy psalms are singing
Away it flies,
Gambolling, stumbling, lightly springing
Before God's eyes.

'Mongst giddypated folk it rambles,
Girls light of mind;
Through forests and through cities gambols
Swifter than wind.

Now in rich raths with jewels glowing
'Mid goodly men;
Now to the ragged pauper going
'Tis fled again.

[1] Meyer, *Ériu*, iii. 13 ff.

Without a boat it skims the ocean,
'Tis swift to fly
Heavenward with unimpeded motion
From earth to sky.

Through all the courses of all folly
It runs, and then
Lightly, untouched of melancholy
Comes home again.

Vain is the hope to hold or bind it,
The unfettered thought
Wanton, unresting, idle-minded,
Sets chains at nought.

The sword's keen edge, the whip's sharp chiding
It scorns, grown bold;
Like an eel's tail it wriggles, sliding
Out of my hold.

No bolt, no bar, no lock, no fetter,
No prison cell
Can stay its course; they serve no better,
Pits deep as Hell.

O fair, chaste Christ! who in all places
Seest all men's eyes
Check by the Spirit's sevenfold graces
Thought's wandering wise.

Terrible Lord of earth and heaven!
Rule Thou my heart!
My faith, my love to Thee be given,
My every part!

So in thy companies to-morrow
I too may go;
Loyal and leal are they. My sorrow!
I am not so.

One so distracted in the oratory would be little likely to
control his vagrant thoughts in the scriptorium. And such
men were the scribes of Irish manuscripts in every age.

The great palaeographer, Traube, assigns five manu-
scripts to Sedulius and his circle.[1] They are these: a Greek
Psalter in the Arsenal Library at Paris (MS. 8451) and the
Gospels in Greek with interlinear Latin version at St. Gall
(MS. 48), both written by Sedulius himself; the Codex
Boernerianus at Dresden, a copy of the Pauline Epistles
(Greek and Latin) also in the hand of Sedulius; the famous
St. Gall Priscian (MS. 904) with Irish glosses and poems;
and the Codex Bernensis at Berne, which contains a text
of Horace's Odes, the Virgilian commentary of Servius,
and some rhetorical works of Saint Augustine (it is a later
transcript of a manuscript of the school of Sedulius). The
variety of subjects in these manuscripts shows the wide
range of Sedulius' interests. But we are concerned only
with the Irish and other marginalia and the inserted poems.
In every case we shall see that these marginal jottings bring
us into a circle which owed a particular devotion to Bridget
of Kildare. This is immediately obvious in the St. Gall
Priscian (probably written in Ireland, or in Wales, and
brought to the Continent subsequently). Bridget is invoked
seventeen times in the margins of that manuscript, while no
other saint has more than seven invocations. That the
manuscript was written somewhere by the sea might be
deduced from a quatrain on one of its pages, written clearly
on some stormy night in a country constantly exposed to
Viking raids:[2]

> The bitter wind is high to-night
> It lifts the white locks of the sea;
> In such wild winter storm no fright
> Of savage Viking troubles me.

The Codex Bernensis quotes a saying attributed to St.
Bridget herself:[3] 'Bridget said: Lowly to the high, mild to
the violent, every man in his turn. Everyone that followeth

[1] Traube, *O Roma Nobilis*, 50 (346).　　　[2] *Thesaurus*, ii. 290.
[3] Ibid., ii. 235.

this counsel, every rough way shall be made smooth before him.' And on another page of the same manuscript we find a touching example of that yearning for their country which has vexed Irish exiles in every age. In the text the scribe has just written a quotation from Ptolemy: 'A man who has gone into a different climate changes his nature in part. But he cannot change altogether, for in his life's beginning the destiny of his body was determined.' And he or another has set his name opposite this passage, 'Cormac', with the pathetic comment: 'So is it always with the Irish who die in a foreign land.'[1] This may recall to us the Horatian line of that other Irish scholar, and, even more vividly, the outburst of Naise son of Uisliu: 'One's own country is better than all; for all good things in whatever measure he hath them are uncomely to a man unless he look upon his country.'

And last we come to the Codex Boernerianus, which Sedulius himself wrote. There is no certain evidence that Sedulius ever went to Rome in his own person, but he tells us in one of his poems that his Muse crossed the Alps with his patron, Hartgar, bishop of Liège, on a journey to Rome. She, perhaps, brought back an unsatisfactory report of what she saw there. The pilgrimage to Rome was the heart's desire of the Irish religious. There is a tale of St. Molua who desired permission to go to Rome from Maedóc, his master. Maedóc put some difficulties in his way and he burst out: *Nisi videro Romam cito moriar*, 'Unless I see Rome I shall not live long'. The verses which we find in the manuscript of Sedulius are of another tenor:[2]

> Who to Rome goes
> Much labour, little profit knows;
> For God, on earth though long you've sought him,
> You'll miss at Rome unless you've brought him.

---

[1] Ibid., ii. 235; *ZCP.* iv. 180.
[2] *Thesaurus*, ii. 296 (and see note).

'Tis frenzy blind,
'Tis witlessness, 'tis madness wild
—Since still to deathward all life tends—
To be unfriends with Mary's child.

These verses too are connected with an incident in the life
of St. Bridget. So that in all these manuscripts the marginalia bring us into the presence of the virgin saint of
Kildare, 'the white lady from Life'. It is a certain conclusion that Sedulius and his friends came from Leinster, a
probable conjecture that they had been educated at Kildare.
There can be little doubt that our wandering Leinster
scholar belonged to their circle. His note-book contains
notes from a commentary on Virgil and quotations from
Augustine and Horace, like the Bernensis; he shows some
knowledge of Greek such as we might have expected to find
in a humbler companion of the Sedulius who wrote the
Arsenal Psalter, the St. Gall Gospels, and the Dresden
Pauline Epistles; he displays the same interest in Irish
poetry as the scribes of all these associated manuscripts, and
the poetry he quotes comes from Leinster, perhaps from
Kildare. The conclusion is irresistible that he was one of
the company of Sedulius. Did he come overseas with them
on that embassy of 848, bringing presents and good words
to Charles the Bald and remain all his life long far from
Ireland among the rough Franks of the Rhineland? It is
very probable that many scholars took the opportunity of
the embassy to fly overseas before the constantly recurring
attacks of the Northmen. And perhaps our scholar and
lover of cats was among them. Did he, one wonders, bring
the kitling with him? And did Pangur the White, that keen
student of mice, share this pilgrimage of philologists?

These scholar exiles came from an Ireland where an
active literary and religious movement had been conditioning the intellectual life of the country for over a century.

The eighth and ninth centuries are the period in which the Irish literature as we know it to-day took shape. In that period the old epic themes were redacted, the native law was intensively cultivated, Latin theology and grammar were the stock studies of the monastic schools, and the traditions of the earlier ages of the Church in Ireland were gathered together in the lives of the saints and other extensive compilations. It is more to our purpose to note that new forms of verse were developed in this time under the Latin influence of the monasteries. For there can be little doubt that the syllable-counting, rhyming verse, the characteristic form of poetry in medieval Ireland, is a creation of this time. And the tendencies of the period visibly influenced the subject matter of that poetry. A study of the theological and hagiographic literature of the eighth and ninth centuries shows that in this, the last age of the old Irish Church, a religious reform was in progress, the essence of which was the intensification of that ascetic spirit which had always marked Irish Christianity. Behind all the activity, all the multifarious production of the time we feel the presence of one spirit, the spirit that causes and sustains all reforms in religion. Reforms come about when men ask themselves with a new urgency: how is the good life to be led? Under the stress of this desperate question they throw aside all the defences of conventional morality, the easy compromises of a merely conforming faith. The mind turns in upon itself and examines the secret springs of its being, the ebb and flow of sense impressions and the response of the spirit to those stimuli which, though they appear to happen within the individual, yet seem foreign to his inner essence. In such periods of a new awareness it is not only in the field of religion that changes happen. Literature also alters front and goes upon a new direction. The individual personality, with its awful responsibilities and strange trivialities inextricably intermingled, takes on a new importance. Pleasure has another meaning and pain is a revelation as well as an agony. Literature, which in the schools always tends to degenerate into a mere social function, feels the stir of a new life and assumes the character of experience and expression. It becomes personal, for the individual soul has now become the centre, the sensitive focus, of all interest. Language ceases to be decorative and ceremonial and grows simpler and more intense so that it almost comes to be the emotion it expresses.

It is thus that I would explain the emergence of personal poetry in Ireland in the period of the religious reform. And under the head of personal poetry I would wish to include that form of composition rather unhappily named 'nature poetry'. For such poetry does not come out of nature, but from the mind of man conditioning natural things by a particular attitude in their presence. Where this attitude fails we get merely descriptive verse, the worst of the many bad kinds of poetry. It was not only that these scribes and anchorites lived by the destiny of their dedication in an environment of wood and sea; it was because they brought into that environment an eye washed miraculously clear by a continual spiritual exercise that they, first in Europe, had that strange vision of natural things in an almost unnatural purity. 'Pleasant is the glint of the sun to-day upon these margins, because it flickers so', writes one at the top of a page of Cassiodorus on the Psalms which he had been copying all winter by the light of a dip candle.[1] It is the emotion, not the sun, that matters here, and the queer impulse that prompts the record. And moved by a like impulse another writes:[2]

> Over my head the woodland wall
> Rises; the ousel sings to me;
> Above my booklet lined for words
> The woodland birds shake out their glee.

[1] *ZCP.* viii. 175.   [2] *Thesaurus*, ii. 290.

That's the blithe cuckoo chanting clear
In mantle grey from bough to bough!
God keep me still! for here I write
A scripture bright in great woods now.

This is the poetry of the *ankerholds* in the woods so charmingly described in the life of St. Déglán of the Déisi:[1]

For he was in his own dear cell which he had built, himself for himself. It is between wood and water in a strait and secret spot on the sea's brink, and a clear stream flows by it from the wood to the sea, and trees gird it beautifully round about.

The anchorite was indeed the characteristic figure of the time, summing up in his person the ideals which inspired the whole movement. Many of the most beautiful poems of the age were clearly born of these anchoritish conditions.

Scholars and ascetics

Quia non cognovi litteraturam introibo in potentias domini.—Ps. lxx. 15, 16.

These Irish scholars who went to the Continent in the ninth century carried with them a passion for learning which had been instilled into them in the Irish schools. There are many witnesses to attest the respect for learning in the early Irish Church. But nothing brings the attitude of the Irish towards scholarship into so vivid a relief as a curious story of the relations between Columcille and Longarad of Ossory, the Augustine of the Gael, which occurs in the notes to the *Félire*.[2]

Longarad Whitefoot: a master in theology, in history, in the Brehon law and in poetry was he. To him came Columcille to be his guest and Lon hid his books from him. So Columcille left a curse on the books: 'May that which thou grudgest be useless after thee,' said he. And so it was, for the books abide still, but no man can read them. Now when Longarad died the men of learning say that all the book-satchels of Ireland fell down

---

[1] Plummer, *VSH.* ii. 58.   [2] *Félire*, 198.

that night. Or rather it was the book-satchels in Columcille's oratory that fell, and Columcille and all they that were with him there fell silent at the noise of the falling of the books. Then said Columcille: 'Longarad is dead in Ossory to-day, the master of every art.' 'May it be long ere that come true!' said Baoithín. 'Unfaith on the man that takes thy office after thee for that!' says Columcille.

Et dixit Columcille:

> Lon's away,
> Cill Garad is sad today;
> Many-familied Eire weeps,
> Learning sleeps and finds no stay.
>
> Lon's no more,
> Cill Garad is weeping sore;
> Learning lies bereft and poor
> All along the Irish shore.

The Annals are full of such laments in verse and prose for deceased learning. *Optimus scriba et anchorita pausavit,* 'a skilled scribe and anchorite he entered into rest', such is the memorial of many a well-spent life; 'learning late deceased in beggary', but the poverty was self-chosen. Here too, however, the old quarrel between the scholars and poets and the ascetics broke out once more. A story that Bede got from Ireland illustrates the eternal antithesis:[1]

In the days of the plague that ravaged Britain and Ireland far and wide the pestilence smote among others a certain scholar of the Irish race. He was a man passionately addicted to letters, but little given to the study of eternal salvation. But when he saw death imminent, he began to be afraid and to tremble lest he should presently die and in requital of his sins be snatched away to the gates of Hell.

The story had a happy ending, for when the case was at its most desperate, the dying scholar repented and an

[1] Bede, *Hist. Eccl.* III. xiii.

English priest who was present with a relic of king Oswald
—a piece of the stake on which the pagans had set the king's
head—cured the repentant scholar with an infusion of this
wood. There are many passages in Irish literature to prove
that this quarrel between letters and religion was clearly
recognized. A curious note in a grammatical tract has a
bearing on the point:[1]

Why is Gaelic called a worldly study and why do the learned
wise make no mention of it? Easily answered: it is because of
all the worldly questions and causes it treats, both of church
and state. Why is the man that studies Gaelic said to be but
a boor in God's eyes? It is not Gaelic at all that is meant here,
but the whole of philosophy: grammar and dialectic and
mathematics, as the poet has said:

> Grammar, learning, glosses plain,
> Even philosophy is vain,
> Arithmetic and letters all
> In Heaven's hall God shall disdain.

But a question: is not Gaelic philosophy? No, indeed, save it
be the pitiful compositions of the authors of the last days whose
aim will be to distinguish themselves above the authors of the
first times. Or the wordly study and idle philosophy is this:
the heresy and unbelief that a man has shown against the truth,
divine and human, and that is the significance of 'a boor in
God's eyes'.

The point that the Irish grammarian is making here is
that certain clerical writers have attacked the rhetorical
studies of the schools as essentially pagan, and Gaelic cannot be identified with these studies except in so far as writing
in it is infected by the same rhetorical devices or is heretical
in tendency. This interpretation of his meaning is con-
sistent with much that we know of the attitude of certain
fathers towards literary and grammatical studies. The
attitude is implicit in Augustine's reference to Virgil: 'What

[1] *Auraicept*, pp. 4-6.

more pitiful object can there be than a man that has no sorrow for his own state, who weeps for Dido dying for Aeneas' love while he has no tears for his own death, the death he died in not loving thee, O God, light of my heart?' It comes out again in Gregory's scorn of grammar and in the mocking question of Sulpicius: 'How shall it profit us to read the battles of Hector and the philosophy of Socrates?' The tale told by Bede is typical of the attitude, and we may find an emphatic expression of it in an Irish quatrain:[1]

> 'Tis sad to see the sons of learning
> In everlasting Hellfire burning
> While he that never read a line
> Doth in eternal glory shine.

A late poem attributed to Columcille—though we may be sure that the sentiments are none of his—once more opposes learning to the religious virtues:[2]

> What woeful folk are they, my friend,
> These clerics at the world's last end!
> In every church this latter band
> Are false to Patrick's high command.
>
> My word it is a goodly word
> Such as from Patrick Éire heard;
> Such Brendan preached; and such the rule
> Of Comgall's and of Ciarán's school.
>
> The saints of Éire long ago
> Wrought miracles this truth to show;
> 'Tis evil done to leave their ways
> For Latin speech in these last days.
>
> For every school will soon, I vow,
> Be following Latin learning now;

[1] *ZCP.* ix. 470; xii. 385.
[2] Hy Many, 119ᵃ; see Flower, *Catalogue*, 75.

Old wisdom now they scorn and song,
And babble Latin all day long.

The best of Latin has no might
To stablish holy Church upright;
We need pure hearts in these bad days,
Piety, charity and praise.

Latin ye love and take no heed
To keep your hearts from evil freed;
But when your Latin speech is done
God's child shall judge you every one!

These poems and quatrains are a scanty gleaning after the great harvest produced by the mysterious impulse of the eighth century which made the Culdee movement in Ireland and was the driving force behind the Irish scholars who did so much for the culture of the Carolingian Empire. The piety was often misguided as the scholarship was erratic and uncertain. But the passion for sincerity of faith and life was as noble in the one as the eager thirst for knowledge in the other. And both of them left on Irish literature an ineffaceable stamp. The study of their own language was pushed almost to grotesque lengths in the Irish schools. But the accurate forms of verse perfected in this period held out for long against the exuberant tendencies developed in Irish prose, and it was only with the decay of the strict metres that the excess of the prose began to deform the verse of the Irish poets. And wherever the verse of the later poets touches personal things, it is always distinguished by an extraordinary sincerity and directness of feeling. It had gone to school with religious emotion when that emotion was quick with the new hopes and the spiritual awakening of an intense and passionate race. The best of these poems are all fire and air, praise and prayer and dedication of the heart, touching little upon dogma or miracle, but content and eager with a new joy and a young revelation. These men ask only to serve and pray, and it is clear that the best reward they ask is to have their praise accepted:[1]

> Lord, be it thine,
> Unfaltering praise of mine!
> To thee my whole heart's love be given
> Of earth and Heaven Thou King divine!
>
> Lord, be it thine,
> Unfaltering praise of mine!
> And, O pure prince! make clear my way
> To serve and pray at thy sole shrine!
>
> Lord, be it thine,
> Unfaltering praise of mine!
> O father of all souls that long,
> Take this my song and make it thine!

Of these scattered fragments of song many are what the English poets of the seventeenth century were wont to term 'Ejaculations', in form single quatrains of simple structure, the inspirations, as it were, of a flying moment of rapture:[2]

> O king of kings!
> O sheltering wings, O guardian tree!
> All, all of me,
> Thou Virgin's nurseling, rests in thee.

So one. And another:[3]

> The maker of all things,
> The Lord God worship we:
> Heaven white with angels' wings,
> Earth and the white-waved sea.

Or again:

> My Christ ever faithful,
> With glory of angels
> And stars in thy raiment,
> Child of the whitefooted
> Deathless inviolate
> Brightbodied maiden!

---

[1] *ZCP.* xii. 297.   [2] *Irische Texte*, iii. 11.   [3] Ibid., iii. 43, § 54.

Sometimes they are prayers:

> Christ keep me safe, Christ guard me lowly,
> Christ bring me to his dwelling high,
> Christ give me strength, Christ make me holy,
> Christ save me lest in Hell I lie.
> In life, in death God keep me whole
> And bless my soul. This hope have I.

Or they commend the Christian way of life, as this:[1]

> A herb unpriced
> I know, good health to win:
> Love thou and fear the Christ
> And hate this world of sin.

Or they take us into the beehive cells of the monks, built of dry stones, each with a cross over the door, gathering within their circular enclosure around the church, the oratory, the refectory, and the school:

> Cells that freeze,
> The thin pale monks upon their knees,
> Bodies worn with rites austere,
> The falling tear—Heaven's king loves these.

The hours of prayer were marked by the striking of a tongueless iron bell which became almost a symbol of the monastic life:[2]

> The clear-voiced bell
> On chill wild night God's hours doth tell;
> Rather in it I'll put my trust
> Than in a wanton woman's lust.

And the striking of this bell, which could only be done under the abbot's direction, was an important function, to be carried out with a grave and stately formality:[3]

> Thou strik'st the bell that calls to prayer,
> The mist dislimns that closed us round;
> Sad cleric! thou art weary there,
> But many listen for that sound.

---

[1] *Gaelic Journal*, iv. 133.   [2] *Irische Texte*, iii. 16, § 40.
[3] *Archiv für Celtische Lexikographie*, iii. 233.

Sweet in Christ's ear the bell's clear voice
Rising from churches everywhere,
And sad souls hear it and rejoice
And in God's house its tone rings fair.

Heaven's hosts make merry when they hear
Its faultless music ringing slow;
Man, woman, child they shake in fear
When the bell hurries there below.

At its chaste cry the devil flies
And hides his sorrow in the sea;
Who hears it when from far it cries
I swear he shall not damned be.

Strike then for God's sake clear and slow
That all the land may hear and come;
This done, God's blessing thou shalt know,
Else in the Judgement look for doom.

They had beautiful epithets for their monasteries: 'Cluain of sweet omen', 'Derry angel-haunted', 'Bangor the chaste and lovely', and the like. And many poems in praise of their churches are found, such as this attributed to Molaisse of Devenish in Lough Erne:[1]

Molaisse sang this:

A goodly land is mine to take,
Hill pastures round the spreading lake,
A church where all the Gael may come,
God the Father's chosen home.

But of all these poems those which deal with the life of the hermits have the most intimate appeal to us. The poets of the old Irish time had always a keen and unaffected delight in the beauty of their country, its hills and rivers, lakes and forests, the cleared plains, and the vast surrounding sea. There was a poet Ruman of the seventh century

[1] *Silva Gadelica*, 33.

whom with a kindly exaggeration they styled the Homer and Virgil of Ireland. We have no means of judging how much or how little he deserved this high style, for none of his poems has come down to us. But a later age made a song for him to sing that shows at least what poetry the eleventh century expected from a poet of the seventh. One detail in the story of this song suggests that he resembled Homer in one point at all events, if we accept the evidence of Horace: *non nisi potus Homerus*. He was singing, the tale goes, to the Northmen of Dublin. The Northmen told him to praise the sea that they might know whether he possessed original poetry. So he praised the sea and he drank the while, saying:[1]

> Tempest on the great seaborders!
> Hear my tale, ye viking sworders:
> Winter smites us, wild winds crying
> Set the salty billows flying,
> Wind and winter, fierce marauders.
>
> Ler's vast host of shouting water
> Comes against us charged with slaughter;
> None can tell the dread and wonder
> Speaking in the ocean thunder
> And the tempest, thunder's daughter.
>
> With the wind of east at morning
> All the waves' wild hearts are yearning
> Westward over wastes of ocean
> Till they stay their eager motion
> Where the setting sun is burning.
>
> When the northern wind comes flying,
> All the press of dark waves crying
> Southward surge and clamour, driven
> To the shining southern heaven,
> Wave to wave in song replying.

[1] *Otia Merseiana*, ii. 79 ff.

When the western wind is blowing
O'er the currents wildly flowing,
Eastward sets its mighty longing
And the waves go eastward, thronging
Far to find the sun-tree growing.

When the southern wind comes raining
Over shielded Saxons straining
Waves round Skiddy isle go pouring,
On Caladnet's beaches roaring,
In grey Shannon's mouth complaining.

Full the sea and fierce the surges,
Lovely are the ocean verges,
On the showery waters whirling
Sandy winds are swiftly swirling,
Rudders cleave the surf that urges.

Hard round Éire's cliffs and nesses,
Hard the strife, not soft the stresses,
Like swan-feathers softly sifting
Snow o'er Míle's folk is drifting,
Manann's wife shakes angry tresses.

At the mouth of each dark river.
Breaking waters surge and shiver,
Wind and winter met together
Trouble Alba with wild weather,
Countless falls on Dremon quiver.

Son of God, great Lord of wonder,
Save me from the ravening thunder!
By the feast before Thy dying
Save me from the tempest crying
And from Hell tempestuous under!

So, too, a little poem quoted in a metrical tractate shows that it was not for nothing that the solitaries built their cells by the sea:[1]

East and by North
Send thine eyes forth

[1] *Irische Texte*, iii. 38, § 24.

> O'er waves with great whales foaming,
> Where sportive seals
> Dance their wild reels
> Through mighty floodtides roaming.

It is of this stern ascetic life, the daily labour and prayer of the monks in their cells and of the anchorites in their oratories, that we learn most in the many beautiful fragments that have come down to us embedded in metrical and grammatical tracts, in commentaries, and on the margins of manuscripts. Reading these strange treatises compiled in a forbidding language modelled on the style of the late Latin grammarians—Priscian, Virgilius Grammaticus, or the universal Isidore—one comes often with a shock of surprise on lyric quatrains delicately wrought, quoted by the learned author to illustrate some point of grammar, metrics, or lexicography. It is as when crossing some dark and inaccessible moorland we stumble suddenly on a hidden nest and out of it a lark springs skyward singing. Thus we find a passage like this introduced to explain the use of a few archaic words:[1]

And so one said:

> The wind over the Hog's Back moans,
> It takes the trees and lays them low,
> And shivering monks o'er frozen stones
> To the twain hours of nighttime go.

That is, the wind is keen when men go to church at Glendalough for vespers and nocturns.

Or, again, take this explanation from the Glossary of Cormac, prince-bishop of Cashel, the earliest as it is the most fascinating of all etymological dictionaries of a vernacular speech:[2]

Ána: these were the little cups set by the wells under the strict

[1] Stokes, *L. B. Félire*, 30 June, p. xcviii, *Trans. R. I. A., Ir. MSS. Ser. I* (1880).   [2] *Anecdota*, iv. 5, § 48.

law. Hence the saying: 'He suffers cups by waters.' And often
they were of silver. So Moccu Cherda sang of Cnoc Raffand:

> The tree-crowned rath on which we stand,
> A bright cup once dipped in its well;
> The ousel's song thrilled all the land
> Here Feeagh Moncha's son did dwell.

That weary travellers might drink from them they set these
vessels by the wells, and the kings put them there to test the
observance of their law.

The commentary on the *Félire*, from which so many of
my examples are taken, abounds in these illustrative quatrains explaining difficult words or obscure allusions. Thus
a hard word has this delightful little poem to illuminate it:[1]

> Learned in music sings the lark,
> I leave my cell to listen;
> His open beak spills music, hark!
> Where Heaven's bright cloudlets glisten.
>
> And so I'll sing my morning psalm
> That God bright Heaven may give me
> And keep me in eternal calm
> And from all sin relieve me.

The extreme antithesis to that ardour of learning which
sometimes, as in the case given by Bede, brought in its
train neglect of eternal salvation was a somewhat unlovely
asceticism. Not to quote the worst examples of the type in
Irish hagiography, one may take a poem from the notes on
the *Félire* which sketches the character of a certain Maeldub, who may be identical with Fintan Maeldub, the successor of Fintan in the abbacy of Clonenagh in Ossory:[2]

> Maeldub, he
> Made the loathly devil flee;
> A sheet, a cloak about him furled
> Was all his having in the world.

---

[1] *L. B. Félire*, 31 Mar., p. lxvi. [2] Ibid., 20 Oct., Comm.

Michael the archangel spake
These good words for Maeldub's sake:
'He since he took the holy vow
Has touched no pillow until now.'

And Michael spoke another word,
—Such praise of mortal ne'er was heard—
'Save Mary's nursling, starry king,
None to men's prayers such fruit can bring.'

Though it should say: 'My back is sore,'
'Twould be not for the weight it bore;
The twisted midge would weary not
To bear all evil Maeldub wrought.

My judgement upon Maeldub here
—Words of a man that knows no fear—
Clutched in his claw the midge could carry
All Maeldub's sins and never tarry!

It would not be surprising if this Maeldub were identical
with the successor of Fintan of Clonenagh, for Fintan was
famous for the severity of his rule. The writer of his life says
of him:[1]

Many from diverse provinces of Ireland, hearing the report
of the religious life of the holy Fintan, came to him and lived
with him under a strict rule. Labouring with their hands after
the manner of hermits they tilled the earth with a hoe. And
rejecting all animals, they possessed not so much as one cow.
And if any offered them milk or butter they received it not.
And did any unknown to the holy Fintan bring milk into the
place, straightway according to the will of the holy man the
vessel was broken by a divine motion. And the straitness of
their conversation being known, none dared to offer them any
flesh.

The aim of this extreme rigour was, doubtless, to render
the fleshly wall so thin that the divine light might shine

[1] Plummer, *VSH.* ii. 98, 102.

through. And the tradition has it that in many cases this aim was achieved. Thus it is related of Fintan:

A certain brother one night hearing that the holy father Fintan was keeping vigil in prayer desired to know in what place he so prayed. And seeking him on this side and on that, he came into the burial place of the holy ones. It was a night of darkness; and the brother gazing at him face to face saw about him an exceeding light spreading far so that his eyes were almost blinded, but God by the grace of the holy Fintan preserved him.

So it is told of other saints that a great light was seen in their cells or descending on them from above, or, most beautiful of all, that it was given to them to fondle the infant Christ. Thus Ita, 'fostermother of the saints', after much fasting and prayer was granted a boon. 'I will accept nought from my Lord,' said she, 'save that he give me his son in fashion of a babe that I may nurse him.' Then came the angel that was wont to do service about her. ''Tis time now,' said she to him. And the angel said to her: 'The boon thou askest shall be granted thee.' And Christ came to her in fashion of a babe. Thus she sang:[1]

> Babe Jesu lying
> On my little pallet lonely,
> Rich monks woo me to deny thee,
> All things lie save Jesu only.
>
> Tiny fosterling, I love thee,
> Of no churlish house thou art;
> Thou with angels' wings above thee
> Nestlest nightlong in my heart.
>
> Tiny Jesus, baby lover,
> Paying good and bad their due,
> The whole world thou rulest over,
> All must pray thee or they rue.

[1] *Félire*, 44–5.

Jesu, thou angelic blossom,
No ill-minded monk art thou;
Child of Hebrew Mary's bosom,
In my cell thou slumberest now.

Though they came my friendship craving,
Sons of princes and of kings,
Not from them my soul finds saving,
But to tiny Jesu clings.

Virgins! sing your tuneful numbers,
Pay your little tribute so;
On my breast babe Jesu slumbers,
Yet in Heaven his soft feet go.

An ascetic practice which led to such exquisite experience as this had an irresistible appeal to the passionate natures of the Irish religious, but there were calmer spirits among them who recognized its dangers. It took shape in an excessive ardour of prayer symbolized in the tale of the saint who stood praying with outstretched arms so long that the birds nested in his open hands; and in that passion of exile that sent so many Irishmen in that day from their home and country. To die in exile with a stranger soil for grave was for the Irish the extreme of abnegation and the crown of the religious life. A series of maxims for the religious in the *Leabhar Breac* gives us the ideal of the ninth century:[1]

If thou be a cleric, be not quick to anger, or loud of voice or covetous. Eat not to fulness, be neither niggard nor liar. Delight not in food.

Thy side half-bare,
Half-cold thy bed!
Thus shall with Christ
Thy praise be said.

An abbot of another kindred over thee. Far from thy kin to thy death day. Foreign soil over thee at the way's end. Know-

[1] Best and Lawlor, *Martyrology of Tallaght*, 110.

ledge, steadfastness, persistence. Silence, humility, chastity, patience. Take not the world's way, good fellow!

The wise counsel of the virgin Samthann of Clonbroney shows that the excess of these tendencies was not un-opposed:[1]

A certain teacher, Tairchellach by name, approached the virgin and said: 'I am minded to put aside study and to give myself all to prayer.' To whom the saint: 'What shall maintain thy mind against straying thought if thou neglect spiritual studies?' And again the teacher said: 'I desire to go overseas on pilgrimage.' And she answered: 'Were God to be found overseas, I too would take ship and go. But since God is near to all that call upon him, there is no constraint upon us to seek him oversea. For from every land there is a way to the kingdom of Heaven.'

And the same saint has a good counsel for those who dispute about the subtleties of devotion:[2]

A certain monk once asked the holy Samthann in what position it were best to pray: lying or sitting or standing. And she answered: 'We must pray in every position.'

Ireland in those days was covered with deep woods, and the hermits were used to build themselves little huts of light construction and live there in companionship with the creatures of the wild. The best picture of this hermit life is given in the life of Ciarán of Saigir, a pre-Patrician saint and the patron of the men of Ossory. Thus the tale goes:[3]

The blessed Ciarán took up his habitation like a hermit in the waste, for all about was a waste and tangled woodland. He began to build his little cell of mean stuff, and that was the beginning of his monastery. Afterwards a settlement grew up by God's gift and the grace of the holy Ciarán. And all these have the one name, Seir.

Now when he came there he sat down under a tree in the shade of which was a boar of savage aspect. The boar seeing

---

[1] Plummer, *VSH*. ii. 260.   [2] Ibid., ii. 259.   [3] Ibid., i. 219.

a man for the first time fled in terror, but afterwards, being tamed by God, it returned like a servant to the man of God. And that boar was Ciarán's first disciple and served him like a monk in that place. For the boar immediately fell to before the eyes of the man of God and with his teeth stoutly severed branches and grasses to serve for the building of the cell. For there was none with the holy man of God in that place. For he had fled to the waste from his own disciples. Then came other animals from the lairs of the waste to the holy Ciarán, a fox, a badger, a wolf and a stag. And they abode with him as tame as could be. For they followed the commands of the holy man in all things like monks.

One day the fox, being more subtle and full of guile than the rest, stole the slippers of the abbot, the holy Ciarán, and turning false to his vow carried them off to his old earth in the waste, designing to devour them there. And when the holy Ciarán knew of this, he sent another monk or disciple, the badger, to follow the fox into the waste and to bring his brother back to his obedience. So the badger, who knew the ways of the woods, immediately obeyed the command of his elder and went straight to the earth of brother fox. He found him intent on eating his lord's slippers, so he bit off his ears and his brush and tore out his hairs. And then he constrained him to accompany him to his monastery that there he might do penance for his theft. So the fox, yielding to force, came back with the badger to his own cell to the holy Ciarán, bringing the slippers still uneaten. And the holy man said to the fox: 'Wherefore, brother, hast thou done this evil thing, unworthy of a monk? Behold! our water is sweet and common to all, and our food likewise is distributed in common among us all. And if thou hadst a desire of thy natural craving to eat flesh, the omnipotent God would have made thee flesh of the bark of trees at our prayer.' Then the fox, craving forgiveness, did penance fasting, and ate nothing until the holy man commanded him. Then he abode with the rest in familiar converse.

Afterwards his own disciples and many others from every side gathered about the holy Ciarán in that place; and there a famous monastery was begun. But the tame creatures aforesaid abode there all his life, for the holy elder had pleasure to see them.

Many of the saints are reported to have maintained such animal friends. Thus Marbán had a pet pig. Moling had a fly, a wren, and a cat. And Keating tells this tale of Mochua:[1]

Mochua and Columcille lived at the same time and Mochua, being a hermit in the waste, had no worldly goods but only a cock, a mouse and a fly. And the office of the cock was to keep the hour of matins for him. As for the mouse it would never suffer him to sleep but five hours, day and night, and if he was like to sleep longer, being weary with vigils and prostrations, the mouse would fall to licking his ear till it woke him. And the fly's office was to be walking along each line of his psalter as he read it, and when he was wearied with singing his psalms, the fly would abide upon the line where he left off until he could return again to the saying of the psalms. Now it came to pass that these three precious ones died soon. And upon that Mochua wrote a letter to Columcille in Alba, sorrowing for the death of his flock. Columcille replied to him and this is what he said: 'My brother,' he said, 'marvel not that thy flock should have died, for misfortune ever waits upon wealth.'

'Methinks', comments the judicious Keating, 'to judge by this jesting of the true saints, they set no store on worldly wealth. How far other is it with the men of to-day!'

Nearest of all to the hearts of the hermits were the birds. The birds, we are told in the *Dindshenchus*, had welcomed Patrick to Ireland. Thus the poet tells the story of how Findloch, 'the white loch', got its name:[2]

> When holy Patrick, full of grace,
> Suffered on Cruach, that blest place,
> In grief and gloom enduring then
> For Éire's women, Éire's men.

[1] Bergin, *Stories from Keating*[3], 35.
[2] *Met. Dinds.* iii. 278; cf. Giraldus Cambrensis, *Itinerarium Cambriae*, Everyman ed. (tr. Hoare), 31.

God for his comfort sent a flight
Of birds angelically bright
That sang above the darkling lake
A song unceasing for his sake.

'Twas thus they chanted, all and some:
'Come hither, Patrick, hither come!
Shield of the Gael, thou light of story,
Appointed star of golden glory!'

Thus singing, all those fair birds smite
The waters with soft wings in flight
Till the dark lake its gloom surrenders
And rolls a tide of silvery splendours.

The hermit poetry is never so lovely as when it has to tell of the bird's song that cheered the scribe at his meticulous labours and the anchorite at his long prayers and vigils. The little poems jet forth as suddenly as the song that prompts them and are as suddenly silent.[1]

The tiny bird
Whose call I heard
I marked his yellow bill;
The ousel's glee
Above Lough Lee
Shakes golden branches still.

Thus one song of the ousel. And another:[2]

He whistles in the willow tree,
Descanting from his yellow bill,
Gold-beaked, black-coated, that is he,
Stout ousel and his trembling trill.

And another:[3]

Sweet ousel chanting blithely there,
Where in the bushes hides thy nest?
Thou hermit no bell calls to prayer!
Thy soft sweet music speaks of rest.

[1] *Irische Texte*, iii. 99.   [2] Ibid., iii. 47.   [3] Meyer, *Bruchstücke*, § 66.

It is told also that the love of the creatures was paid by love again. There is a saint, Maelanfaid of Dairinis, of whom we are told little, and of that little this charming tale is most fragrant in memory:[1]

Maelanfaid abbot of Dairinis, a cell of Mochuda's Lismore, placed where Blackwater runs into the sea. This is that Maelanfaid that saw one day a little bird weeping and making moan. 'O my God,' said he, 'what has befallen the creature yonder? Now, I swear,' said he, 'that I will eat no food until it be revealed to me.' So abiding there he beheld an angel coming his way. 'Hail, cleric!' says the angel, 'let the trouble of this vex thee no longer. Molua, Ocha's son, is dead. And for this cause the creatures lament him, for that he never killed any creature, little or big. And not more do men bewail him than the creatures, and among them the tiny bird thou seest.'

The Irish, indeed, could not imagine an earthly or a heavenly paradise, a pagan or a Christian Elysium, that did not echo with the voices of birds calling to the hours. A tenderness steals into the formal verses of the schools as they describe the Tree of Life in which the birds of heaven sing. So in the *Saltair na Rann*, in which a tenth-century poet retold the bible story in verse that keeps usually to the mnemonic level, the words remember an accumulated beauty of tradition when they come to treat of this matter:[2]

> The Tree of Life with bloom unchanged,
> Round it the goodly hosts are ranged,
> Its leafy crest showers dewdrops round
> All Heaven's spreading garden-ground.
>
> There flock bright birds, a shining throng,
> And sing their grace-perfected song
> While boundless mercy round them weaves
> Undying fruit, unfading leaves.

[1] *Félire*, 56. [2] *Saltair na Rann*, 613 ff.

A lovely flock! bright like the sun,
A hundred feathers clothe each one,
And pure and clear they chant together
A hundred songs for every feather.

This is the song of which another poet has to tell:

The singing birds of Heaven greet
The Virgin's son with music sweet;
One whisper of their song would heal
The agonies damned spirits feel.

And it was perhaps one of these birds of the Tree of Life
that, in the Irish form of the universal medieval legend,
lulled Mochoe of Noindruim into his mystic slumber:[1]

Mochoe of Noindruim slept a sleep
With flesh unwithered, long and deep,
Till of the folk he knew of old
Remained but skulls upon the mould.

A little bird from Heaven cries
And lulls that goodly man and wise,
And in that place three strains he hears,
And every strain was fifty years.

It was to this heaven, beautiful with meadows and alive
with the song of birds, that the Irish ascetics hoped to come
after their austerities. It is characteristic of their way of
thought that they are willing to express their ideal through
the lips of an inspired madman. We are told of practically
every Irish saint that he lived in an intimate converse with
lepers and people of troubled wits. As Moling had Suibne
Geilt, so Cummíne Fota had Comgán Moccu Cherda, the
fool of the Déisi, for his companion. These madmen, the
legend related, roamed the woods, living in the treetops
and sharing their couches with the creatures of the wild.
They could go under the water and take the fishes in their
hands. Their utterance was a medley of obscure folly and

---

[1] *Félire*, 158.

inspired wisdom. If one part of their mind was dim from the quenched reason, another part was illuminated by the divine light. The tales of them are wild and strange, and much of the most beautiful poetry of the time is associated with them.

So it is given to Moccu Cherda to tell of Heaven:

Moccu Cherda sang this:

> The heavenly sky
> Where Christ the son of Mary is,
> There if he die a man lives still
> And whatsoe'er he will 'tis his.

I make no doubt that some, in reading this account of the ideal of these Irish religious expressed by their poets, have been reminded of the histories of St. Francis and those among his early disciples who most nearly realized his precepts. I, at least, have constantly had that beautiful story in mind, and as a pendant to all that has been written above I shall venture to add the passage from Giovanni Parenti's *Sacrum Commercium* that tells how the Lady Poverty came to be entertained by the brethren:

Now when all things were made ready they constrained her to eat with them. But she: 'Show me first,' said she, 'the oratory, the chapterhouse, the refectory, the kitchen, the dormitory, the stables, the goodly seats, the polished tables and great habitations. For none of these do I see, but I see you cheerful and happy, overflowing with joy, fulfilled with consolation as though ye deemed that all things ye ask shall be granted to you.' And they answered and said: 'Our lady and our queen, we thy servants are weary from the long way, and thou journeying with us hast had no small toil. Wherefore let us eat together first, if thou wilt, and all things shall be fulfilled at thy behest.' 'I will do what ye say,' said she. 'But now bring water that we may wash our hands and napkins that we may dry them.' So they made haste and brought forth half an earthen vessel full of water, for they had not a whole one. And pouring the water on her hands they looked on this side and on that for a napkin. And finding it not, one of them offered her the tunic he had on to dry her hands with. And she taking it magnified God with all her heart for that he had brought her among such men. Then they brought her to the place where was a table made ready. And being come thither and seeing nought but three or four crusts of bread of barley and of bran laid upon grass, she made great marvel within herself, saying: 'Who ever saw the like in all the generations? Blessed be Thou, O Lord God! who hast care for all, Thou hast power to do all thy will and Thou hast taught thy people by such deeds to find grace in Thy sight.' And so they sat down together giving thanks to God for all His gifts. Then the Lady Poverty bade them bring cooked food on dishes. And, behold! one dish was brought full of cold water that all might dip their bread in it. For they had no plenty of dishes, no superfluity of cooks. She begged that at the least a few fragrant herbs might be set before her all uncooked, but having no gardener and knowing nought of a garden they gathered wild herbs in the woods and set them before her. And she said: 'Bring me salt to lend a savour to the herbs, for they are bitter.' 'Wait, Lady,' said they, 'till such time as we may go into the town and bring it for thee, if there be any to give it to us.' 'Give me a knife,' said she, 'that I may trim off what is not needed and cut the bread, for it is very hard and dry.' They say to her: 'Lady, we have no iron-smith to make us knives. For this time use your teeth for a knife, afterwards we will make provision.' And she said: 'And have you a little wine?' And they answered saying: 'Lady, we have no wine, for the first thing for man's life is bread and water, and it is ill done for thee to drink wine, for the spouse of Christ should flee wine like poison.'

Now when they were filled, taking more joy in lack than they would have done in abundance of all things, they blessed God in whose sight they had found such abundant grace and they brought her to a place where she might rest, for she was weary. So she cast herself down uncovered on the bare ground. And she asked for a pillow for her head. And straightway they brought a stone and put it under her head. Now she slept a peaceful and a quiet sleep and rose up after a short space and asked them to show her their monastery. And they brought her to a certain hill and, showing her all the world that might be seen from thence, they said: 'This is our monastery, lady!'

We might easily imagine this tale told of the Irish communities, of the folk of Fintan of Clonenagh or of Maelruain of Tallaght. If the Irish had had the telling of the tale, it would have worn a wilder air, and we cannot doubt that it would have had a savour of that ironic humour which goes hand in hand with the simplicity and clear mysticism of their legends of the saints. There would have been the singing of birds in it, perhaps, and they would scarcely have left out their dumb friends of the wood. But it would have had the same ending, for the Irish religious made the whole world of Europe in their day into their monastery. But, to adapt the saying from Ptolemy in the Codex Bernensis, though they went into a different climate and perhaps changed their nature in part, change altogether they could not, for in their life's beginning the destiny of their minds was determined.

III

THE RISE OF THE BARDIC ORDER

THE Book of Leinster, a manuscript of the twelfth century, contains the only private letter in Gaelic that has come down to us from the pre-Norman period. It is fortunate that just this letter has been preserved, for its contents are of great importance for the history of the Irish manuscript tradition and of Irish poetry. It runs thus:[1]

Life and health from Find, Bishop of Kildare, to Aed mac Crimthainn, professor of learning to the high king of the Southern Half, successor of Colum mac Crimthainn [in the abbacy of Terryglass], chief shanachie of Leinster in wisdom and knowledge and practice of books and learning and study. Write out for me the conclusion of this little story.

> Be sure of this, keen-witted Aed,
> Rich in the holy wealth of song,
> Be thou long time or short away,
> I always for thy coming long.

Send me the songbook of Mac Lonáin that I may understand the meaning of the poems therein, *et vale in Christo*.

It is a charming letter, bringing vividly before our eyes those industrious monks to whom we owe the preservation of the early literature of Ireland. It is clear that the manuscript that we know as the Book of Leinster—or some part of it—was then a-writing in Terryglass on the commission of the Bishop of Kildare (who died in 1160), and was being sent as written to the bishop for his approval. In another place it is written that Aed wrote the book, collecting its material out of many books. Of these sources some must have come originally from Tallaght in County Dublin; others, there is reason to believe, came from Clonmacnoise, which lies higher up the Shannon to the north of Terryglass.

[1] Atkinson, *The Book of Leinster*, introduction, p. 7.

Clonmacnoise was the *cathair Chiaráin*, the *civitas Ciarani*, the monastic city of St. Ciarán, the patron saint of the men of Connacht. Terryglass itself was placed upon the shores of Loch Derg, and across the lake lay the territories of Hy Many and Aidne. Fland mac Lonáin, for whose poems the bishop asks, was the great poet of Aidne, a descendant like Cléireach, the ancestor of the O'Clery clan of poets, of Guaire, the famous king of that territory, and he counts in the tradition as one of the three chief poets of Connacht. It was natural to suppose that his poems would be treasured at Terryglass, for, if a tradition recorded in a manuscript in the British Museum speaks truth, he and his family were buried there. The following note is appended to a poem attributed to him in this manuscript:[1]

Fland mac Lonáin, ollave of Éire, sang this composition the day after his slaying, and he was buried in Tulach Mochaime in the midst of Terryglass, himself and his son and his father and his mother, Lathóg, and three of the kings of Muskerry with them, as he related in this quatrain:

> Under Mochaime's flags we lie,
> Six goodly warriors dead;
> Stout men were we, but that passed by,
> Above our bones men tread.

He is the first professional poet of Ireland of whom we have any definite tradition, and it is to him and to his followers in the tenth century, Mac Liag and Mac Coisse, that the later bards look back as to their great exemplars. The three poets are brought together in a curious tale in the Connacht manuscript, the Yellow Book of Lecan. This tale explains the origin of a poem on the place-names of Slieve Aughty, the range of hills that runs westward from Loch Derg on the western border of Hy Many:[2]

Three bards in chief there were of Connacht: Mac Liag,

---

[1] Flower, *Catalogue*, 480.   [2] YBL. facs. 195ª1.

Mac Coisse and Fland mac Lonáin, that is, God's son, man's son and devil's son. Fland mac Lonáin, devil's son was he, he was so satirical and burdensome, for he never left a house without some idle satire. And Mac Liag was man's son, for he kept good cheer in his house and he was a goodly man himself. Mac Coisse was God's son for his exceeding charity, and he died on pilgrimage.

Now Ilrechtach was the name of Mac Liag's harper and he had been Fland's harper before and Mac Liag had him after Fland's death. Mac Liag went his way to converse with Brian, and Ilrechtach went with him. He would often go that way from Loch Ree south over Aughty to Limerick, taking twelve bottles with him with what he needed of food in them. For there are twelve sights in Aughty and he was wont to drink a bottle at each sight of them. Now on a time they went south and they sat them down on a certain hill that had to name Ceann Crocháin, and Mac Liag said: 'Many hills and lochs and high places are there here and 'twere a great knowledge to know them all.' Said Ilrechtach: 'Were but Mac Lonáin here, he would have the knowledge of every one of them.' Said Mac Liag: 'Take him and hang him up.' Ilrechtach begged a respite till morning and 'twas granted him not to be hanged till then. He fasted that night and the soul of Fland came to succour him. When they rose in the early morning on the morrow they saw Mac Lonáin coming towards them and he said to them: 'Let your captive go and I will tell you the tale of every high place that is in Aughty.' Thus was the harper saved from hanging at Mac Liag's hands and Mac Lonáin spoke this poem there: 'Lovely, lovely! lofty Aughty', etc.

This tale is very characteristic. Fland, it will be seen, was a great posthumous poet, and he must have practised his art under difficulties, for the poem in the Museum manuscript tells us that he went to hell when he died, though it is only fair to his reputation that another tradition reports him as speaking from heaven. His punishment is a reward for the avarice of 'the devil's son', a trait prominent in all the tales about him. The Museum poem tells how he gathered wealth by his song, and there is another poem attributed to his mother Lathóg, herself a poet, in which she warns him against using his art for the purpose of extortion. He is thus in the tradition a kind of foil to his ancestor Guaire, king of Aidne, the accepted pattern of liberality. This characteristic gives a sardonic point to a tale in which the God of Poetry plays upon his lack of hospitality very neatly. This tale too is found in the Yellow Book of Lecan.[1]

On a time it befell that Fland mac Lonáin was in an empty house, he and his band, and they had no food, for their serving folk had gone from them. There came a great rain and wild weather upon them and they said, one to another: 'We would not leave here to-night if we had food, for it is an evil day.' They were speaking thus when they saw a clodpoll of savage aspect with a bill-hook in one hand and in the other a beef. They asked him would he sell the beef. He said he would in return for a cow of his own choosing. Mac Lonáin said he would give him a cow if he were allowed time for it. The clodpoll said he would give him time. 'Give us the beef now,' said Mac Lonáin. 'You shall have it,' said the clodpoll, 'only let me slaughter and cook and dispense it.' 'By my art,' said Mac Lonáin, 'you should be paid a price for that.' 'I ask nought,' said the clodpoll, 'but my cow to be given me according to the promise.' 'You shall have it for sure,' said Mac Lonáin. The clodpoll slaughtered the beef then and flayed and seethed it and dispensed it when it was ready, and he gave his due share to each man of them and they were grateful. Every good thing came to them, and in whatsoever way any wished for aught, in that way was it given him. So the clodpoll went from them and at the year's end he came again with four others in his company, every man of them with a billhook in his hand. Rude and rough were those five, they needed great room and much food, their manners were evil and they beat the women, the hounds and the gillies in the house and pro-

[1] *Anecdota,* i. 45.

claimed that they would accept nothing but a cow always in milk or they would stay in the house for ever until they got that cow. Then Mac Lonáin asked the fellow his name. Said the clodpoll: 'Woodman son of Barked Wood am I,' said he. And then Mac Lonáin made this lay: 'Woodman Barked Wood's son is here', etc.

Then said the clodpoll: 'That is the cow I sought, for poetry is ever in milk. And I am Oengus in Mac óg that have come to thee.'

This tale is a good example of the allegorical compositions of the bards. There is a play in it on the two meanings of the word *fid*, 'wood' and 'letter'. Thus the name the god assumes, Fidbadach mac Feda Ruscaig, might mean either 'Woodman son of Barked Wood', or in the literary language 'Man of Letters son of Poetic Letter', with another play on *rúsc* 'bark' and *rosc* 'declamatory poem'. The moral of the fable is that poetry, though the study that leads to it has a forbidding aspect, is in the end a rich reward, a cow that never goes dry, in the pastoral image of the Irish bard.

And the method employed by Oengus and his band to enforce their claim hoists the poet with his own petard. The god drives home the lesson of Fland's mother, Lathóg of Tyrconell:[1]

> My blessing and my counsel take,
> My son and Aidne's glory Fland:
> Be generous for your honour's sake,
> Since men give all that you demand.
>
> Believe your mother's word that still
> The niggard poet's in the wrong;
> Give of your riches with good will,
> You ask rewards from all for song.

Fland died by violence in the Decies of Munster, appar-

---

[1] Meyer, *ZCP*. viii. 109.

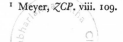

ently in the year 893. The Four Masters are eloquent in his praise:[1]

> Fland mac Lonáin, the Virgil of the Scotic race, chief poet of all the Gael, the best poet of Ireland in his time, was slain by the sons of Corr Buide (they were of the Uí Fothaith) at Loch dá Chaoch in the Decies of Munster.

And, as we have seen, he was buried in the great monastery of Terryglass with the kings of Muskerry, a Connacht bard with royal folk of Munster.

I have dealt at some length with Fland mac Lonáin because he is at once a representative of the older order of Irish poets and yet stands in a close relation with poets who seem to mark a new departure. We have very little evidence as to the earlier poets. Much of the matter that has come down to us relating to their character and organization appears to have passed through the hands of their successors and to have been retouched in the process. One very striking fact on which perhaps sufficient stress has not been laid is their almost complete absence from the Annals. Down to the tenth century there is poetry in the Annals, but there are very few poets. Ruman mac Colmáin is practically the only poet whose death is chronicled in this early period. But much space is given to the deaths of men of learning—*sapientes, philosophi, scribae*, and the like. The Annals were compiled in the monasteries and it is, of course, not unnatural that first place should be given to those representatives of literature with whom the monks were best acquainted. But if the poets really played a prominent part in that organization of the national literature which, as we have seen, was a striking feature of this period, it is certainly curious that their deaths should not be recorded in the Annals. Such glimpses as we get of them—of Senchán Torpéist, of Dallán Forgaill, and their fellows—show them wandering about the country and haunting the courts of

[1] *Annals of the Four Masters*, i. 548.

the kings, attended by a band of followers, with a panegyric in one hand and a satire in the other, mercenaries of the God of Poetry as the *fiana*, the roving warrior bands, were mercenaries of the God of War. But we do not get the impression that they were during the early historical period the chief literary force in the country. That force centred in the monasteries and all the evidence goes to show that, whatever part the poets played in the oral preservation of the tradition, its written record was the work of the church. At this early period the church must be taken to mean the separate monastic establishments, each serving the religious and educational needs of its own district, and the whole held together rather by personal associations than by the tie of a stringent centralized ecclesiastical organization. It is probable that the means of writing, the manufacture of vellum, and the developed scribal art, were to be found only in these monasteries and their schools. All our existing early manuscripts were written in monasteries and they derive from earlier, lost manuscripts which, so far as we can trace their origin, also had a monastic source. Moreover, it is certain that the literary orthography of Old Irish was settled by the clerics. No evidence has ever been produced to prove the existence of writing for literary purposes in Ireland before the coming of Christianity. The study of early Irish literature, so far as that study rests upon documents, is therefore dependent on a valuation of the existing monastic antiquities, and it is perhaps better to postpone theories as to prehistoric origins until that very considerable field of research has been sufficiently exploited. When this study has been concluded it will be possible to distribute the parts played respectively by the clerics and the lay poets without injustice to either party. We may be sure that the clerics were no passive transmitters of the traditions recited to them by the poets. They had their knowledge of the current Latin literature; they had their conceptions of the course of world history and their own idea of the way in which Irish tradition might be adapted to those conceptions; they taught in their schools the Latin rhetoric of the Dark Ages. All these preconceptions must have profoundly modified the original matter, and we can only hope to get back to that original matter by the gradual isolation of these imported elements. The scholars working in the monasteries it must have been who built up all that curious fabric of the *senchas*, the genealogical and historical lore of Ireland which was henceforth to dominate the historical work of the schools. A good example of their work is the *Lebor Gabála*, the Book of Conquest, the *Landnámabók* of the Gael. This work grew up by a gradual accretion in the period between the sixth and the twelfth centuries. It was in a sense a propagandist work, designed to gather into one whole the history, traditions, and mythological origins of the various races of Ireland, free and unfree alike. The result is a strange medley of poetic history, mythology, folklore, and biblical and classical reminiscence, a characteristic product of these 'masters in theology, in history, and in poetry'.

It became canonical in the schools and its teachings were faithfully reproduced down to the seventeenth century. Thus, in that last rally of the poets of Ireland, the Contention of the Bards, Lughaidh O Cléirigh, the poet of the north, accuses Tadhg mac Bruaideadha, protagonist of the south, of controverting the teaching of that almost sacred book:[1]

> The right of Heber, though impugned by you,
> The Book of Conquests proves it and 'tis true;
> I marvel not thou giv'st that book the lie,
> Since even Scripture's truth bad men deny.

So Domhnall Ó Súilleabháin of Béara appeals to the king of

---

[1] McKenna, *Contention of the Bards*, i. 54, qq. 14–15.

Spain on the ground of their ancient relationship, a claim
based upon the claim of the *Lebor Gabála* that the Irish came
from Spain. And when this Domhnall's son Diarmuid died
in Spain, Eoghan Ó Dálaigh, the poet, wrote thus in his
elegy:[1]

> To match the weeping born of Béara's pain
> A tender kindred weeping sounds from Spain:
> True tears are those that on a distant strand
> Fall for the sorrow of another land.

So does century reach out a hand to century, and the
learned invention of history's morning hours become an
instrument of high policy in its meridian.

The relations between the monastic men of letters and
the poets must have been close and they were sometimes
uneasy. In the lives of the saints the poets are usually
represented in a somewhat unfavourable light. They are
called 'mimes and histrions' (*mimi et histriones*) or *jongleurs*
(*joculatores*) and they constantly appear as extorting gifts
under the threat of a satire. A curious tale, The Proceedings
of the Burdensome Bardic Company, which, though we
have it in its full form in a late version, yet rests upon earlier
material, is one long riotous attack on the poets and their
ways. On the other hand, another tale, The Vision of Mac
Con Glinne, takes up the case of the poets against the monks,
though, as we shall see, the arrow is winged with a feather
of the bird it strikes.

Mac Con Glinne, the hero of this amazing composition,
is represented as studying at Armagh. This is how he is
introduced:[2]

Anier mac Con Glinne, he was a great scholar, very knowledgeable. He was called Anier because of his way of making
panegyrics and satires. And it's no wonder he had that name
Anier (i.e. Nonrefusal) for there was none before or after him

---

[1] O'Grady, *Catalogue*, 399–400.
[2] Meyer, *Aislinge Meic Con Glinne*, 9.

whose satires and panegyrics were so burdensome, and that's why he was called Anier because there was no refusing him. The scholar conceived a great desire to take to poetry and give his studies the go-by. For he had had too much of the life of learning. So he turned it over in his mind where he should go on his first poet's round. And the fruit of his research was this: to go to Cathal mac Finguine who was then on his king's round in Iveagh of Munster. For the scholar had heard that there was enough and to spare of every sort of white meat for him to get there. And he had a hungry lust after white meats.

Mac Con Glinne, it will be seen, is an example of the type of truant scholar, the *scholaris vagans* of European literature, the happy-go-lucky vagabond who goes singing and swaggering through the Middle Ages until he finds his highest expression and final justification in François Villon. If in some place apart from time 'François Villon, escollier' and 'Mac Con Glinne, the great scholar, very knowledgeable' could meet together, they would understand one another well enough, and the talk between them (it would be, of course, in Latin) would be worth going out of time to hear.

The tale that follows is one long parody of the literary methods used by the clerical scholars. At every turn we recognize a motive or a phrase from the theological, the historical, and the grammatical literature. A full commentary on the Vision from this point of view would be little short of a history of the development of literary forms in Ireland. And it is not only the literary tricks of the monks that are held up to mockery. The writer makes sport of the most sacred things, not sparing even the Sacraments and Christ's crucifixion. He jests at relics, at tithes, at ascetic practices, at amulets, at the sermons and private devotions of the monks; the flying shafts of his wit spare nothing and nobody. It is little wonder that the monks were at odds with such poets as this. The point of the whole composition is the contempt of the monk for the poet and the way in which the poet turns the tables on him. There is a burlesque exaltation of Mac Con Glinne throughout, and it culminates in the testimony to his worth given by the devil: 'Thou art a man with the grace of God, with great knowledge, with keenness of intellect, with fervency of humbleness, with the desire of every good thing, with the grace of the sevenfold Spirit.' It is probable that the monks would have agreed as to the keenness of intellect and the desire of every good thing in the poets; they would certainly have thought that only the devil could have attributed humbleness and the grace of the Holy Spirit to them.

The Vision in the form in which we have it can hardly be earlier than the twelfth century, but the conditions it reflects certainly go back to an earlier period. It at once sums up and turns into gigantic ridicule the learning of the earlier time much in the same way as François Rabelais at once typified and transcended the learning of the later Middle Ages. Basing ourselves then upon these texts, we shall be justified in distinguishing three types among the Irish literary men of the classical time. There were the *sapientes*, clerics or laymen, attached to the monastic schools; their truant scholars who gave learning the go-by and took to poetry; and the poets themselves, going singly or in bands about the country with their satires and panegyrics, levying their tribute. There were quarrels enough between the three classes, but they must have worked together often enough under the liberal conditions of the society of those days. And the literature in the great twelfth-century manuscripts is, no doubt, the fruit of their co-operation.

The existing manuscripts of Ireland fall naturally into three groups. The first group is constituted by the theological and grammatical manuscripts in Latin with Irish glosses (and sometimes, to our great profit, with Irish poems) either written on the Continent or carried thither in the eighth and ninth centuries. So far as the origins of these manuscripts can be determined, they would seem to emanate from the schools of Leinster and south Ulster and to reflect the teaching in those schools. One manuscript of the early ninth century, the Book of Armagh, which contains continuous Irish texts and glosses, comes as its name imports from Armagh, and is still in Ireland. Another manuscript, the Stowe Missal, which also contains a continuous Irish text and rubrics in Irish was the mass book of Tallaght near Dublin, and is now in the possession of the Royal Irish Academy. It is curious that after many wanderings it should have come to rest almost in the place where it was originally written. *Habent sua fata libelli!* The rest of these eighth- and ninth-century manuscripts are on the Continent or, like the Southampton Psalter in St. John's College, Cambridge, in England. The contents alone of these manuscripts would show that they were written by clerics.

The next group of manuscripts appears in the eleventh–twelfth-century period. It consists of purely religious manuscripts like the two Books of Hymns and manuscripts of a mixed character like *Lebor na hUidre*, the Book of Leinster, and the Oxford manuscript known as Rawlinson B. 502, which contain both secular and sacred texts, the secular writings often based on lost manuscripts of the eighth and ninth centuries. The transcribing of the manuscripts is still in the hands of the clerics, but we notice that the literary centre of gravity, if one may use the term, has now shifted westwards. The two manuscripts which we can certainly place, *Lebor na hUidre* and the Book of Leinster, were written in religious houses on the reach of the Shannon between Loch Ree and Loch Derg, Clonmacnoise and Terryglass. The Rawlinson manuscript was also written at Clonmacnoise. For reasons which I shall discuss later it is probable that this prominence of the western scriptoria is not accidental, due to a chance preservation of manuscripts from that district. At present it is mainly important to note that the writing of manuscripts is still in the twelfth century the monopoly of the clerics.

The third group comprises the majority of Irish manuscripts written on vellum before the seventeenth century and the great paper manuscripts of that century. The first difference here is in the scribes. These are no longer clerics (with some exceptions to be explained later, p. 116 f.). They are a new class of men, the hereditary bards attached to the noble families of Ireland, whether the families of the old Gaels or those Anglo-Norman lords who came afterwards to be known as the Old Foreigners. These literary families were the guardians of the tradition as it was arranged and stored in the older manuscripts by the scribes of the great clerical schools. And we cannot understand the history of the Irish tradition until we establish with some certainty how, when, and where these families came into their position, and in what way and in what localities they took up the task bequeathed by the clerics. I think that it is possible to arrive at certain probable conclusions in this matter. But before we enter on the discussion of this difficult question I will take the opportunity to illustrate the continuity of the tradition from the clerics to the hereditary scribes from another point of view.

The *Leabhar Breac* is a vast compilation of chiefly theological contents transcribed by the Mac Egans in the late fourteenth century in that same district between the two great lakes of Shannon in which *Lebor na hUidre* and the Book of Leinster were written. The contents for the most part date back to the twelfth and earlier centuries and it is thus, in a sense, despite the lateness of its transcription, a sister book to those two great collections. It contains, however, a few writings, chiefly poetical, of a later period, and it is interesting to observe in these how happily and with what art the tradition of the direct, personal poetry which is the glory of the early monastic period of Irish literature maintains itself into the new time. The most famous religious poet of medieval Ireland was Donnchadh Mór Ó Dálaigh, who died in the Abbey of Boyle in MacDermot's country in 1244. There is a poem attributed to him in our manuscript and, for its delicate humour and intimate pleasure in bird life, it might have been written by one of the early hermits. It runs thus:[1]

> Wrens of the lake, I love them all,
> They come to matins at my call,
> The wren whose nest lets through the rain,
> He is my goose, my cock, my crane.
>
> My little bard, my man of song
> Went on a foray all day long;
> Three midges were the poet's prey,
> He cannot eat them in a day.
>
> He caught them in his little feet,
> His brown claws closed about the meat;
> His chicks for dinner gather round,
> Sure, if it rains they'll all be drowned.
>
> The crested plover's lost her young,
> With bitter grief my heart it stung;
> Two little chicks she had—they're gone:
> The wren's round dozen still lives on!

Of the same period, or perhaps somewhat later, is another poem in the book, treating with a poignant reality a theme which, whether spontaneously or by one of the many modes of derivation, is common to the literatures of most countries:[2]

> Sadly the ousel sings. I know
> No less than he a world of woe.
> The robbers of his nest have ta'en
> His eggs and all his younglings slain.
>
> The grief his sobbing notes would say
> I knew it but the other day:

[1] Meyer, *Gaelic Journal*, v. 40.   [2] Knott, *Irish Syllabic Poetry*, 29.

Sad ousel, well I know that tone
Of sorrow for thy nestlings gone!

Some soulless lout of base desire,
Ousel, has turned thy heart to fire;
Empty of birds and eggs thy nest
Touched not the cruel herdboy's breast.

Thy young things in the days gone by
Fluttered in answer to thy cry.
Thy house is desolate. No more
They chirp about the twig-built door.

The heartless herders of the kine
Slew in one day those birds of thine;
I share that bitter fate with thee,
My children too are gone from me.

Till night they hopped among the trees,
Chicks of the bird from overseas,
Till the net's meshes round them fall.
The cruel herdboy took them all.

O God that made the whole world thus,
Alas, thy heavy hand on us!
For all my friends around are gay,
Their wives and children live to-day.

Out of the fairy hill a flame
To slay my hapless loved ones came:
No wound is on them, but I know
A fairy arrow laid them low.

So in my anguish I complain
All day for wife and young ones slain:
They go not out and in my door,
No marvel my sad heart is sore!

There is an intense note of personal feeling in this poem.
One might otherwise have supposed it composed upon a
hint from Virgil. Homer in the Odyssey thus describes the
weeping of Odysseus and Telemachus:

Shrilly they cried with wails more loud than those of birds, sea eagles or crooktaloned vultures whose young the hunters have taken, all unfledged.

With this passage in his mind Virgil tells of the sorrow of Orpheus for lost Eurydice:

> So in the poplar shade
> Weeps her lost young the sorrowing nightingale
> Whom the rude ploughman marked and all unfledged
> Stole from the nest. She, perched upon a sprig,
> Weeps nightlong and renews her song forlorn,
> And the wide woodland echoes her sad cry.

An Irish poet might well have known this passage from the *Georgics*, for one of his fellows in this period was engaged in translating the *Aeneid* into prose. But the simile is so natural that there seems little need to suppose a borrowing. So in the fourth act of *Macbeth* Shakespeare needed no suggestion from the classics to depict almost in the same terms as the Irish poet the incredulous sorrow of Macduff for the loss of his wife and children:

Macduff. My children too?
Ross.   Wife, children, servants, all
     that could be found.
Macd.   All my pretty ones?
     Did you say all? O, hellkite! All!
     What, all my pretty chickens and their dam
     At one fell swoop . . .
     I cannot but remember such things were
     That were most precious to me. Did Heaven look on
     And would not take their part?

To the medieval Irishman and the poet of Jacobean England it may well have wanted no help but from the deep feeling of their own hearts to see some failure of Heaven's justice in a sudden doom overtaking the bird-like swiftness and innocence and delight of young children. In the same way other themes beloved of the monks who made the early religious literature passed over into the new time. We have seen the poet Fland mac Lonáin returning from hell (or from heaven) to succour his distressed harper. So in the earlier manuscripts there are many stories of souls returning from their punishment in the after world to warn their friends of the inevitable consequence of sin. These tales are usually based upon the motive known to all the Middle Ages as the 'Trental of St. Gregory', and it is from Hell that the tortured soul comes with warning. But in a poem from a fifteenth-century manuscript in the British Museum (Add. MS. 30512) the call of friendship reaches to heaven and troubles the peace of the blessed there. This manuscript was written by the well-known scribe William Mac an Legha, apparently in Desmond, and contains amid much other matter certain texts drawn from the collections of Clonmacnoise. The present poem is one of these. It is perhaps of the fourteenth century and tells of the sorrow of Niall O'Sheridan, late abbot of Clonmacnoise, for a friend, Murchadh, who had in some way violated the solemnities of the Mass. Niall is represented as appearing in a vision to one of the community of St. Ciarán and bidding him intercede for the imperilled soul of Murchadh:[1]

> Go to God's house in grief and rue
> And there his holy nocturns do:
> Ask the fair angels there that dwell
> To keep my Murrough safe from Hell.
>
> I am Niall that once so lightly leapt,
> Strictly the monkish rule I kept
> And got in guerdon Heaven's joy fair
> Till Murrough's peril found me there.
>
> Here in this place the house of God
> One day my lightsome footstep trod:
> Until he come to join me here
> I shiver for his soul in fear.

[1] See Flower, *Catalogue*, 478, § 16.

May Murrough's ear take this my speech
And to his understanding teach:
They that the holy offering curse
Fare ill in life and after worse.

All men between the earth and sky
—Upon my soul I tell no lie—
If they the holy offering spurn
Shall, dying, in Hell's smother burn.

Go, tell my tale to those that pray
At the high sacrifice each day,
For if thou tellst not, thou shalt be
To Mary's son an enemy.

Go, tell the priest that offers Christ,
Unless he hearken, he shall see
His own salvation sacrificed
And under God's displeasure be.

To those familiar with the ruling tone of the poetry of Ireland in the later Middle Ages these verses come like a voice out of the old world, that world of the dreaming anchorites in their woodland solitudes and the diligent scribes in their narrow cells in which the personal poetry with which I dealt in my last chapter took its rise. For in the Middle Ages poetry in Ireland was a function of the State almost as much as in the communistic or corporative constitutions which afflict the modern world. We shall see in the next chapter something of the work of the professional poets. I am here concerned to make the attempt to determine under what conditions the curious institution of the bardic order as we know it in the Middle Ages arose, and how it came into possession of the jealously guarded traditions of the monastic period.

Down to the twelfth century, we have seen, the manuscripts which survive, or of which we have any tradition, were written in, or in association with, the old monastic houses and by clerics. From that time onwards they are written by a special order of lay scribes. How and where did this change come about? The chief centres of the older literature were in eastern and southern Ireland, in southeast Ulster, in Leinster, and in Munster. But the great manuscripts which concentrate that earlier tradition were written in monasteries in central Ireland, such as Clonmacnoise and Terryglass placed on Shannon's middle course between Loch Ree and Loch Derg. Partly because of the Norse occupation of the eastern seaboard and partly for other reasons this process of the shifting centres had been going on between the ninth and the eleventh centuries. From the late twelfth century the tradition thus concentrated within the limits of a small district of central Ireland was propagated by a class of hereditary literary families. And when we come to trace the genealogies of these families we find that the most important of them all derive from this same district. The O'Mulconrys, the O'Clerys, and the O'Duignans were the chief transmitters of the historical and genealogical tradition. The O'Mulconrys and the O'Duignans were of the families of Westmeath whose chief monastery was Clonmacnoise, while the O'Clerys came from the district of Hy Many, on the other bank of the Shannon, which also acknowledged Clonmacnoise as its patron house. The law scribes of medieval Ireland were the MacEgans, also of the Hy Many, whose chief seat was in northern Tipperary on the shores of Loch Derg. The O'Dalys, the chief poetic clan, were again of the peoples of Westmeath. These families, cradled in central Ireland, gradually scattered throughout the country in the Middle Ages, carrying their traditions with them. Many of the families kept the record of their dispersion. A curious and characteristic story shows us the way in which the O'Dalys came to Argyllshire and the Isles of Scotland. Of that whole race of poets none left a deeper mark in tradition than two brothers, Donnchadh Mór, the religious poet, styled by the Four Masters 'a poet who never was and never will be surpassed', who died in 1244 and was buried in the abbey of Boyle in Roscommon, and Muireadhach of Lissadil. The tale of Muireadhach is told by the Four Masters under the year 1213. In that year a tax-gatherer in O'Donnell's service, one Finn O'Brollaghan, went from Donegal into Sligo to levy O'Donnell's taxes in that district. He came first to the house of this Muireadhach at Lissadil. Here he fell into altercation with the poet and insulted him, twenty times, says Muireadhach, when once would have been enough for most people. O'Daly took the course natural to an incensed poet and, seizing an axe, cut O'Brollaghan down. It was an extraordinarily sharp axe, say the Four Masters, and one blow sufficed to finish the tax-gatherer. Anticipating a not unnatural anger in O'Donnell at this insult, O'Daly fled for refuge to the Norman, MacWilliam Burke, in Galway. He addressed a poem from this refuge to O'Donnell in which he detailed the circumstances and expressed some surprise at the way in which the chieftain was taking a very trivial incident:[1]

> What reason for such wrath can be?
> The rascal bandied words with me.
> I took an axe and hewed him down—
> Small matter for a prince's frown.

O'Donnell, however, proved implacable and hunted O'Daly out of Galway into Thomond and afterwards to Limerick. The citizens of Limerick, under threat of a siege, sent the poet away, and he came at last to Dublin. O'Donnell returned to Donegal, but later in the year went to Dublin and forced the retreat of the harried poet to Scotland. There he remained until at last a series of poems mollified the wrath of his irascible lord, and O'Daly returned to Ireland. During his stay in Scotland he appears to have

[1] *Studies*, xiii. 241–6.

gone to the Holy Land, for poems of his still exist written in the Adriatic on his way to the East.

Why did he go there? He left Ireland in 1213. In 1215 Innocent III was preaching the Fifth Crusade, which got under way in 1217. The assault was to be delivered by way of Egypt, and the armies of Europe beleaguered Damietta on the eastern delta of the Nile. The capture of that strong place was the only achievement of the crusade. While the armies lay before Damietta, St. Francis came to the camp in the vain attempt to make peace between the warring worlds. There was a Scottish contingent with the European forces, and it may well be that Muireadhach Ó Dálaigh was with them. It is difficult otherwise to explain his presence in the Levant. It is a thrilling thought that the Irish poet may have seen the great founder of the Order which was later to have so profound an effect on Irish literature. There is no stranger possibility in history than the chance that these two passed one another among the tents on the shores of Egypt—the kinsman of the greatest religious poet of Ireland and the Tuscan saint, whose children were to transform the religious poetry of Europe and of Ireland. I like to imagine them meeting—strange figures both— looking wonderingly and unknowingly on one another and going by in ignorance to their several destinies.

There is a poem of Muireadhach Ó Dálaigh's, written on shipboard in the Adriatic, no doubt upon this very crusade, in which he tells how, as the ship tosses, his thoughts go back to Ireland:[1]

> How peaceful would my slumbers be
> In kind O'Conor's fair demesne,
> A poet in good company
> Couched upon Éire's rushes green.

His wish was granted him and he died in Ireland, but not before he had founded that kindred of the MacVurichs

[1] O'Grady, *Catalogue*, 337–8.

who more than any other race of bards maintained the Irish tradition in Scotland.

Thus by the end of the tenth century the old ecclesiastical tradition had concentrated in the centre of Ireland, and from that same district the chief of the lay families who were to carry on that tradition through the Middle Ages derived their origin. Now it happens that just at this period this district, the heart of Ireland, was under the influence of a powerful king whom the later men of letters claimed as the founder of their order. This was the famous Brian Bóroma. He came of the Dalcassians of Clare, originally an obscure clan whose importance dated from not long before his time. Munster was ruled from Cashel by the kings of a people named the Eoghanacht. Brian in the late tenth century displaced the rulers of this race in Cashel, and by the year 1000 had established himself in the high kingship of Ireland. His power depended largely upon an alliance with O'Kelly of Hy Many, whose seat of kingship was at Athlone, commanding the passage of the Shannon into Connacht, and with a congeries of peoples who held the territories along the east bank of the river. To consolidate this alliance he moved his chief seat from Cashel to Kincora on the Shannon above Limerick, and that place became for a time the political capital of Ireland. In the year 1005 he went on a circuit of Ireland to affirm his position. On that circuit he came to Armagh, the metropolitan city of St. Patrick, and there his secretary wrote in the famous Book of Armagh an acknowledgement by Brian of the ecclesiastical supremacy of the abbot of Armagh as primate of Ireland. In this note Brian is described as *imperator Scotorum*, 'emperor of Ireland'. In other places he is called the Augustus of the Western World. These two titles, *imperator et Augustus*, were the style of Charlemagne as Holy Roman Emperor. And there can be little doubt that Brian conceived himself as performing the functions of a Charlemagne in Ireland. Charlemagne was the typical civilizing ruler of the early Middle Ages, and his influence was an inspiration to all Europe. He consolidated his peoples and gave them laws in his capitularies; and his influence counted for much in the great movement of culture which we know as the Carolingian Renaissance. Alfred of England is an outstanding example of this type of culture-king. He codified the laws, he inspired the compilation of the *Anglo-Saxon Chronicle*, he translated works of scholarship and theology from the Latin and encouraged the native poetry.

And in all these regards Brian conforms to the type. There had been an active study of the ancient laws in Munster in the ninth century under Cormac mac Cuilennáin, the most learned king of the Eoghanacht line. There is evidence that the commentary on the *Senchus Mór*, the central code of the law, dates from Brian's time. The Book of Rights, which codified the tribute system of the Irish constitution, drawn up under Cormac, was recast at Brian's court. Down to Brian's time history in Ireland was a matter of bare skeleton Annals. The Munster Annals of Innisfallen, though not departing from this scheme, grow fuller in detail in his days; and the record of his exploits, the Wars of the Gael and the Gall, assumes for the first time in Irish historiography the proportions of a chronicle. Poetry was vigorously cultivated at his court. By the ninth century the system of rules which governed Irish metrics and the poetic rhetoric had been codified in a series of treatises. These treatises, it can be proved, were finally redacted at Brian's court and formed into the system which henceforward was to govern the practice of the poetic schools. In every department of literature there are definite evidences of a new activity in his reign. It would not be surprising if the doctrine of the later schools that they date from his time were true. But there is no contemporary record of the institution, and the literary families first appear in the Annals about 1200, though their origin must go back farther than that. It is perhaps safest to conclude that the institution was of gradual growth, but that it finally consolidated and established a tendency which had begun to manifest itself in his day and under his influence.

The impression made by Brian upon his own generation is best expressed in the almost contemporary chronicle, The Wars of the Gael and the Gall, where, after recording his victories over the Norsemen and his triumphant circuit round Ireland, the chronicler indites a eulogy:[1]

So Brian returned from his great royal visitation around all Ireland and the peace of Ireland was proclaimed by him, both of church and people, so that peace throughout Ireland was made in his time. He fined and imprisoned the perpetrators of murders, trespass and robbery and war. He hanged and killed and destroyed the robbers and thieves and plunderers of Ireland. . . . After the banishment of the foreigners out of all Ireland and after Ireland was reduced to a state of peace, a lone woman came from Tory in the North of Ireland to Cliodhna in the South, carrying a ring of gold, and she was neither robbed nor insulted.

> From Tory to pleasant Cliodhna
> Carrying with her a ring of gold
> In the time of Brian, the bright, the brave,
> A lone woman made the circuit of Ireland.

By him were erected the noble churches of Ireland and their sanctuaries. He sent professors and masters to teach wisdom and knowledge and to bring books from beyond the sea, because the books and writings, in every church and in every sanctuary where they were, were burned and thrown into the water by the plunderers; and Brian himself gave the price of learning and the price of books to everyone that went on this service. Many works also and repairs were made by him. By him were erected the churches of Killaloe and the church of Iniscealtra and the belltower of Tomgraney and every other

[1] *Cogadh Gaedheal re Gallaibh*, 136.

work in like manner. By him were strengthened all the duns and fastnesses and islands and celebrated round forts of Ireland.

This is the typical eulogy of a culture-king in a Europe emerging from the Dark Ages. Thus Bède has this praise of Edwin of Northumbria:[1]

Such was the peace in England in those days so far as the rule of Edwin extended that, as the proverbial saying goes in our day, even if a lone woman with her newborn child should desire to make the circuit of the whole island from sea to sea, she could do it, and none would offer her injury.

Bede goes on to say that Edwin caused bronze cups to be hung by the wells that passers-by might drink from them. This same detail is found in Irish in the ninth-century Glossary of Cormac. William of Malmesbury also has a variant of this latter tradition with reference to King Alfred:[2]

He diffused such peace throughout the country that he ordered golden bracelets which might mock the eager desires of the passersby, while noone durst take them away, to be hung up on the public causeways where the roads crossed each other.

It is probable that the theme is of Scandinavian origin, for Saxo Grammaticus has a similar story of Frotho, the mythical peace-king of the two Scandinavias:[3]

Frotho, now triumphant, wished to renew peace among all nations that he might ensure each man's property from the inroads of thieves and now ensure peace to his realms after war. So he hung one bracelet on a crag which is called Frotho's Rock and another in the district of Wig after he had addressed the assembled Norwegians, meaning that these bracelets should serve as a test of the honesty which he had decreed.

---

[1] *Hist. Eccl.* III. xvi.

[2] *Gesta Regum Anglorum* (ed. Stubbs), 130; cf. *Flores Historiarum*, attributed to 'Matthew of Westminster' (ed. Luard), i. 471.

[3] *Saxo Grammaticus*, v (ed. Holder), 164; tr. Elton, 202.

The application of this theme to Brian shows that he was regarded as a king of the type of Frotho, Edwin, and Alfred, one who restores peace and gives laws to his people and rules with a strong hand in an ordered realm. Under his sway the devastation which had been wrought by the Vikings was repaired and the old literary tradition was revived and reinforced. It is little wonder then that the poets looked back to his reign as a kind of new birth of literature and credited him with the institution of that order of the shanachies who, when the old tradition of the churches threatened to fail in the dangerous days of the English invasion and the introduction of new orders of monks and friars from abroad, preserved the old tradition for the later generations.

In the fourteenth century two poets fell at odds over the question whether the Shannon belonged chiefly to Connacht or to Munster. The Connacht bard rightly claimed that his province possessed the fountain and the major part of the course of the great river. But the Munster poet countered with the prevailing name of Brian who had made Shannon into a name synonymous with poetry:[1]

> Shannon! King Brian's native river,
> —Ah! the wide wonder of thy glee—
> No more thy waters babble and quiver
> As here they join the Western sea.
>
> By ancient Borivy thou flowest
> And past Kincora rippling by
> With sweet unceasing chant thou goest,
> For Mary's babe a lullaby.
>
> Born first in Breffney's Iron Mountain
> —I hide not thy nativity—
> Thou speedest from that northern fountain
> Swift through thy lakes, Loch Derg, Loch Ree.

[1] Knott, *Irish Syllabic Poetry*, 21.

Over Dunass all undelaying
Thy sheer unbridled waters flee;
Past Limerick town they loiter, staying
Their flight into the western sea.

From Limerick, where the tidal welling
Of the swift water comes and goes,
By Scattery, saintly Seanán's dwelling,
Thou goest and whither then who knows?

Thomond is clasped in thy embraces
And all her shores thou lovest well,
Where by Dunass thy cataract races
And where thy seaward waters swell.

Boyne, Siuir and Laune of ancient story,
And Suck's swift flood—these have their fame;
But in the poet's roll of glory
Thine, Shannon, is a nobler name.

IV

THE BARDIC HERITAGE

THE strange order of lay poets, historians, and lawyers whose function it was to transmit and develop the tradition of Irish literature in the Middle Ages may have come into existence as a result of the policy initiated by Brian Bóroma at the beginning of the eleventh century. The Annals begin to record the deaths of members of these families early in the twelfth century. Cú Chonnacht na scoile Ua Dálaigh of Bunbrosna in Westmeath died at the monastery of Clonfert, the house of St. Brendan, in 1139. From his grandson Aengus are descended all the O'Dalys of Ireland. A Tanaidhe Ua Maelchonaire died in 1136, and in the Gospels of Maelbhrighde Ua Maeluanaigh, written at Armagh in 1138, there is a poem by Néidhe Ua Maelchonaire, a member of the same family, who were historians and poets to the O'Conors and MacDermots and other related families of Connacht. In the same year died Amlaibh Mór mac Firbhisigh, whose family were the literary men of the other great people of Connacht, the Hy Fiachrach of counties Mayo and Sligo. Later in the twelfth century we find such names as Mael Íosa Ó Dálaigh, *ollave* of Ireland and Scotland, who died in 1185, and Raghnall Ó Dálaigh, dead in 1161. From about 1200 the literary families are firmly in the saddle, and in describing that unique phenomenon, the bardic order, one is at liberty to select material from five centuries, for their constitution and outlook remained substantially the same throughout the Middle Ages, although it will appear that certain modifications of subject-matter were introduced from external sources in the course of that period.

The history, the organization, and the productions of the bardic poets in the Middle Ages have been admirably dealt with by Professor Bergin, Dr. Quiggin, and Miss Knott, and the religious poetry which was one department of their activity has been edited by Father Lambert McKenna. I do not propose to repeat here the excellent exposition of these things by scholars better equipped than myself. I will only select one or two points which may serve to illustrate their way of life and the continuity of tradition which it was their function to preserve.

The poems which have come down to us, preserved in part in the *duanaires*, the poem-books of the noble families, or in the collections such as those written in Flanders in the great dispersion of the seventeenth century, are in great part eulogistic compositions couched in a traditional rhetoric and illustrated with allusive stories taken from older legends, from classical sources or from the *exempla* books of the preaching friars, of which I shall have something to say later on. To be a poet in medieval Ireland was to be an expert in the exact and happy employment of this rhetorical speech and a master of the various branches of historical and genealogical allusions which diversified the substance of the bardic compositions. The manuscripts which have come down to us from this time are to a large extent the text-books used in the poetic and historical schools, and from them we can form a fairly complete estimate of the nature of their studies. It is more difficult to represent to ourselves the actual daily life of these academies and the manner in which the students proceeded through their terms. Our best source of information on this matter is the Introduction to the *Clanricarde Memoirs*, published in London in 1722. This account has been printed by Dr. Bergin with illustrations from the texts.[1] To his account I can only add the name of the anonymous author, who can be proved to have been Thomas O'Sullivan, a Tipperary man who haunted Lord Harley's library in the

[1] Bergin, *Journal of the Ivernian Society*, v. 156 ff.

seventeen-twenties. It is clear that the old tradition lingered long in Tipperary, and O'Sullivan's description can be trusted. He explains that poetry was an hereditary profession, and that the students gathered in some remote place far from the resort of people, and worked in a large structure divided up into cubicles each furnished with a bed, lying upon which in complete darkness they composed their poems on themes set by the master. The poem composed, lights were brought and they wrote it down and presented it to the masters for criticism in the main place of assembly. For week-ends and holidays they were entertained by the gentlemen and rich farmers of the neighbourhood, who also provided the provisions for the subsistence of the school. They worked only from Michaelmas to the first of March and the full course lasted six or seven years, 'which', says O'Sullivan, 'you will the less admire upon considering the great difficulty of the Art, the many kinds of their Poems, the Exactness and Nicety to be observed in each, which was necessary to render their numbers soft, and the Harmony agreeable and pleasing to the Ear'.

So between November and March the poetic scholars pursued their mysterious task, mastering the poetic language, the management of the complicated metres, and the *seanchus*, the accumulated lore of Irish history and legend. Behind the formal parade of the great manuscripts in which this curiously assorted learning is stored we can dimly discern the students at their work and catch here and there an echo of their laughter as they played. Probably many of the jesting quatrains found in the manuscripts of the early modern period go back to the later Middle Ages and reflect the playful or angry contentions of the schools. Down to modern times in Ireland it has been accounted a necessary accomplishment of a poet to compose verses impromptu, an easy gift to those trained in the long rigours of the bardic schools. There is a tale of two poets, Éamonn

Ó Caiside and Matha Ó Luinín who fell at odds. Matha
said some bitter thing which is unrecorded and Éamonn
countered thus without a moment's hesitation:

> A good mate's Matthew,
>   But not to pass the bottle;
> Uprising or downsitting,
>   God's curse in Matthew's throttle.

That was apparently enough for Matthew, for no answer
is recorded. Another such impromptu is attributed to the
famous sixteenth-century poet, Tadhg Dall Ó Huiginn.
It is said to have been his first composition and so may well
belong to his student days. He was clearly at issue with a
fellow student who pretended to poetry, a claim which
Tadhg ironically admits:[1]

> Yon spark's a poet, by my troth!
> Sprat and whale are fishes both;
> All birds build nests; so, like the rest,
> We call the tit's wee lodge a nest.

There is a curious instance of these controversies in a
poem by Fearghal Óg Mac an Bhaird, one of the poets of
Donegal, who ended his days in misery and destitution at
Louvain, the refuge of so many Irish men of letters in the
seventeenth century.[2] He appeals in his misery to Florence
Conry, the founder of the Irish College of St. Anthony there,
and reminds him of an ancient friendship between their
families which owed its origin to one of these contentions of
the schools. When Florence's grandfather was a lad in one
of the poetic schools he challenged another student to a
contest in poetic art. Perhaps he was a little doubtful of
his own powers, or maybe the kindred of his competitor was
too well represented in the school. At all events before the
test he made his way from Roscommon to Donegal and

---

[1] Knott, *Bardic Poems of Tadhg Dall Ó Huiginn*, i. xxiv.
[2] *Studies*, viii. 72.

besought the poetic clan of Mac an Bhaird to help him.
That whole clan, says Fearghal, set forth on a 'family
visit' and triumphantly vindicated the young O'Mulconry
against his rival. Since that day there had been a friendship between the families. These associations of the schools
were no doubt a powerful factor in that close intimacy
between the men of letters of medieval Ireland which
maintained the tradition of subject and treatment un-
impaired for so many centuries and protected the poetic
dialect against the infiltrations of localisms in phonetic and
idiom. When the student had spent seven terms in the
school he was eligible for the degree of *ollave*, and, pos-
sessing that degree, he might seek a chieftain to serve. We
have a poem by Eochaidh O'Hussey, written in the sixteenth century, in which he tells us that he has been studying in Munster and cannot make up his mind whether to
stay in the haunts of learning in the South or return to his
native Fermanagh and the service of his chief Maguire.[1]
The hesitation is, of course, assumed in order to give him
an opportunity of painting the irresistible delights that over-
sway his judgement and draw him to the North. They are
the pleasures often depicted in these compositions. In the
limewashed castle the gracious chieftain will be awaiting
him, thronged round by his nobles, with their eager lances
and gleaming swords; the poets will be chanting eulogies
in the hall to the voice of the sweet harps; horses with
pointed hoofs curvetting round the shining walls; ladies
weaving embroideries on cloth of gold; crimson pennons
fluttering at the lance-point; on the cattle-besprinkled hill
above the lake with its boats the shouting of the hunters,
the sweet cry of the horn; the friendly people of the clan
gathered to the feast in the hall that needs no other light
than the flaming of the jewels on the drinking cups; and
above them all the chieftain himself like the sun shining

[1] Knott, *Irish Syllabic Poetry*, 72.

over that joyous company. No, the odds are too heavy, so farewell to Munster and its learning and hail to Fermanagh and its lord. O'Hussey, we know, returned, and in another poem he instructs Maguire in the duties of a chieftain to his *ollave*.[1] He expounds the ancient doctrine according to which a king, a bishop, and an *ollave* have a like dignity. To his *ollave* a king must give his best of love, his richest gifts, the precedence in the council, the seat of honour at his shoulder, the half of his bed, and all conceivable immunities. O'Hussey's art, he says with complacency, is tempered and attuned by all the cunning craftsmen, north and south, his learning is the honey of true bees. So that he demands no more than his right, he does not hold with reversing institutions. And to support his dignity he must have an estate convenient to the castle, well found with arable and pasture and waste. So found and equipped, he will be in a position to give counsel to his master and to serve him in all the functions of a poet.

The poet thus established in the service of a master would devote himself enthusiastically to his interests and was of necessity and choice an upholder of the monarchical principle in its most extreme form. A poem in a fifteenth-century manuscript asserts the two complementary doctrines, that a king should be strong and that his subjects should yield him perfect obedience:[2]

> If you have a feeble king
> Or him offend in anything,
> On the rich earth it bodes ill
> And works confusion in your will.
>
> Lugh's great bow, Finn's noble heart,
> Alexander's royal part,
> Trojan Hector's weapons bright,
> Achilles' prowess in stern fight;

[1] See O'Grady, *Catalogue*, 475.　　　[2] *ZCP*. xii. 385.

Croesus' riches famed of old,
Lovely Orpheus' harp of gold,
Absalom's own steadfast skill,
Pharaoh's indurated will;

Strength of Manoa's long-haired son,
The wise heart of Solomon,
Octavian's sway o'er lands and seas
And the might of Hercules;

If these glories, I aver,
Gathered in one mortal were,
His deeds, his valour all were vain,
Did no king above him reign.

He that will not serve on earth
His own king of noble worth
Shall find not at the end of things
Mercy from the King of kings.

The latter years of the fourteenth and the first half of the
fifteenth century saw the production of a series of great
manuscripts in central Ireland and in Connacht, compiled by members of the literary families and embodying
the secular and ecclesiastical learning which they inherited
from the monastic scribes. These manuscripts—the Book
of Hy Many, the Yellow Book of Lecan and the Great Book
of Lecan, the Book of Ballymote, and the *Leabhar Breac*—
recorded the old tradition, and they were followed in the
course of the fifteenth and sixteenth centuries by a second
series of books which embodied the developing literature
of the later Middle Ages. Of the later literature some
account will be found in the next chapter. From the native
tradition which here undergoes a recasting intended to
bring it into line with the taste of the new age we may select
one important section for fuller treatment. The Ulster
Cycle of Conchobor and Cú Chulainn was the product of
the heroic age of Irish literature, that time between the
seventh and the ninth centuries when king and monk and

poet co-operated in a passion of memory and creation to build up the legend of the Irish past. That other cycle of story, the tale of Fionn and his companions, which through the strange parody of Macpherson was destined to win the ear of Europe for Celtic literature, began to be recorded in the same period, but its full development in the form in which we know it belongs to this bardic time of the later Middle Ages. It is as characteristically romantic as the Ulster cycle is characteristically heroic.

From the eighth century down, tales and poems about the *fiana*, the wandering war-bands most famous of which was the company led by Fionn mac Cumaill, had been in circulation in all parts of Ireland, but no attempt had been made to gather these floating traditions into a larger whole comparable with the *Táin Bó Cuailnge* and its attendant cycle of tales. This was the task which some unknown genius of the thirteenth century essayed. By the same literary device which we have seen in use to authenticate the historic cycle of which the tale of Fionn is properly a part, he imagined that certain of the *fiana* had escaped the ruin of their fellows and had encountered St. Patrick on his missionary journeys through Ireland. In response to his eager questionings, their spokesman, Caoilte or Oisín, summons up old memories and broods with a noble melancholy over the heroic past. They travel together round Ireland, and everywhere dead heroes and vanished scenes revive again in story and poem, and the saint instructs his scribe to write them down that they may give pleasure to companies and nobles to the world's end. So comes into being the work known as *Agallamh na Senórach*, the Colloquy of the Ancient Men. It is marked off sharply in tone and manner from the older epic tradition and begins already to show all the characteristics of the bardic age. Many of the stories and poems had certainly existed before, but here they are wrought into a loose unity, and the text so constituted was to have a profound influence on the further development of the theme. For now this Fionn saga became the favourite theme of the story-tellers and the poets and their audience. The old heroic tales were still remembered and some among them were rewritten after the fashion of the new time. But the living, developing theme of the medieval period in Irish literature is the tale of Fionn. And here the style and matter of the *Agallamh* are dominant. The tradition divided into two branches. Old tales were rewritten and new ones composed in prose with metrical insets, and out of the poems in the *Agallamh* grew the Ossianic lays of the later time. The prose tales drop the convention of the dialogue with St. Patrick, but it is usual, though not obligatory, in the lays. Oisín is now the interlocutor, and the poems are commonly known to us as Ossianic lays. But a curious change in the tone of the dialogue appears in the later period. In the *Agallamh* the relation between the saint and the heroes is one of perfect courtesy. They defer to him and he is tender to their pagan memories. But in the later lays the opposition of pagan and Christian sentiment is more sharply conceived. The hero and the saint rail upon one another in good set terms. The extreme expression of this conflict is in the quatrain which the Irish-speaking peasantry of to-day still declaim with a peculiar pleasure:

If I saw God and Oscar hand to hand on a hill, were I to see Oscar down, I would say that God is a strong man.

This is not, as some have thought, evidence of a pagan reaction or of medieval anticlericalism; it is with the poets who composed and the peasants who repeat the poems merely the delight in developing the implications of a situation to their last extreme. A number of these later lays were collected at the end of the period into a new metrical colloquy, which appears frequently in modern manuscripts. This may well remind us of the *Geste of Robin Hood*, which appears to have been put together with additions from earlier ballads, but there is this difference that, while Robin Hood according to Child is absolutely 'a creation of the ballad muse', Fionn and his companions are, as we have seen, heroes of old time with a long tradition behind them.

It is difficult to sum up in a few words the effect of this developing theme which so many generations have so fondly cherished. Here I will only call attention to one or two points in which Macpherson fails to catch its prevailing note. From first to last, from the circumstances of its origin and transmission, it is the expression of a people whose occupation and whose joy are the fight and the chase. It is without subtlety, without sentimentality, and the memories that come back to Oisín in his old age are not the ghosts of old time, but the living companions of his youth summoned up by a powerful spell to range the battle again and again to follow the chase through the gusty glens and over the bald mountain summits of all Ireland. There is much convention, but the reality behind the convention is that active life under the sky and all the environment of hill and wood and plain and sea, the shouting of men hard beset, the cries of the birds and beasts as they follow in the hunt. Natural things are seen here as they appear to a hunting people, to men who look long into the depth of a wood where the invisible deer lies couched, or hear the birds cry as they lie waking at either end of sleep in a mountain bivouac. A late poem of the cycle says:[1]

These were the joys of the comely son of Cumall—to hearken to the cry upon the Red Ridge, to slumber by the fairy hill of Assaroe, to hunt the lands of Galway of harbours. The warbling of the ousel of Letterlee, the beating of Rury's wave against the strand, the belling of the stag of Moy Maoin, the call of the

---

[1] Ó Donnchadha, *Filidheacht Fiannaigheachta*, 42.

fawn of Glendamhail. The clamour of the hunt on Slieve Grot, the noise of the stags about Slieve Gua, the gull's scream yonder in Irrus, the raven's shriek above the hosts. The ship making music with the wave, the wolfpack howling in Drumlis, the hound Bran speaking in Cnoc na nDall, the splashing of the three torrents on Slieve Mis. The note of the horn at the hunt's end, the beagle's cry on the Fians' hill, the feast in Allen among the poet companies—these were his joys for everlasting.

These too were the joys of the chieftains and poets of medieval Ireland, and the passing of them is the theme of many a lament of the seventeenth century. The tales and poems which tell of these battles and hunts, of adventures by flood and field, of the *fiana* defending Ireland against foreign invasion, of their strange relations, now friendly, now inimical, with the fairy people of the hills, and finally of the twilight of the heroes and their last fight against odds —this is the true romantic saga of medieval Ireland and the chief gift of the poets to their country. And this too is the one surviving heroic theme in folk-lore to-day. Conchobor and Cú Chulainn are forgotten names, or at most a vague tradition of antique greatness. But wherever Irish survives as a living tongue, old men kindle at the mention of Fionn and Oscar and Diarmaid and Goll, and at the slightest provocation will begin upon the long tales which the fond folk-memory still loyally preserves.

Some years ago I was wandering idly one day along a road upon an island which lies three miles out into the Atlantic beyond the most westerly point of Ireland. The island is entirely Irish in speech, and the older inhabitants still preserve a rich treasure of song and story. As I strolled along I heard a call from the next field, and clambering over a wall, I found myself in the presence of an old man of over eighty years, who yet retained something of the strength and happy spirit of his youth. As I came up he spoke: 'You have an unsociable way with you (*Tá cuma fhiadhain ort*). Don't you give folk a greeting when you go by them on the road?' 'Yes,' I said, 'I greet people. But I didn't see you over the wall.' 'A man should have his eyes in every corner', he said. 'But sit down now and we'll have a crack together.' He had been digging potatoes in a furrow of the field, and he now laid the potato spade cross-wise over the furrow and, sitting down on one end, courte-ously signed to me to take my place on the other end. I did so and, without further preamble or explanation, he fell to reciting Ossianic lays. For half an hour I sat there while the firm voice went steadily on. After a little while he changed from poetry to prose, and began to recite a long tale of Fionn and his companions and their adventures throughout the world, how they came to Greece and what strange things befell them there. At times the voice would alter and quicken, the eyes would brighten, as with a speed which you would have thought beyond the compass of human breath he delivered those highly artificial passages describing a fight or a putting to sea, full of strange words and alliterating rhetorical phrases which, from the tradi-tional hurried manner of narration, are known as 'runs'. At the end of one of these he would check a moment with triumph in his eye, draw a deep breath, and embark once more on the level course of his recitation.

I listened spellbound and, as I listened, it came to me suddenly that there on the last inhabited piece of European land, looking out to the Atlantic horizon, I was hearing the oldest living tradition in the British Isles. So far as the record goes this matter in one form or another is older than the Anglo-Saxon Beowulf, and yet it lives still upon the lips of the peasantry, a real and vivid experience, while, except to a few painful scholars, Beowulf has long passed out of memory. To-morrow this too will be dead, and the world will be the poorer when this last shade of that which once was great has passed away. The voice ceased, and I awoke out of my reverie as the old man said: 'I have kept you from your dinner with my tales of the *fiana*.' 'You have done well,' I said, 'for a tale is better than food', and thanked him before we went our several ways.

In such memories, and in an odd quatrain still surviving from the byplay of the schools, the tradition of the poets is still alive in the spoken tongue. And in the great manuscripts written in the schools of poetry and history and law we can see them busy at their task of preserving the old tradition which their order had been instituted to guard. They stood firmly over the ancient ways and had but small capacity of adapting themselves to the change of times. Their existence was bound up with that of the aristocratic order which they served, and with it they fell. But their memory and their influence lived after them and, if the spoken Irish of to-day is perhaps the liveliest, the most concise, and the most literary in its turns of all the vernaculars of Europe, this is due in no small part to the passionate preoccupation of the poets, turning and re-turning their phrases in the darkness of their cubicles and restlessly seeking the last perfection of phrase and idiom.

V

IRELAND AND MEDIEVAL EUROPE

WE have now to consider the tradition as it was affected, chiefly in the Later Middle Ages, by borrowings from external sources. The medieval period in Irish literature may be taken as extending from the twelfth to the seventeenth century and even in certain survivals to the present day. This period has been somewhat neglected by writers on Irish literature, and has been only sporadically represented in published texts. The reason of this neglect is, no doubt, to be sought in the motives which have hitherto prompted those who have for one purpose or another taken up the study of the literature. Thus the linguists, approaching the study at first from the side of comparative philology, naturally applied themselves primarily to the oldest monuments of the language. It is only of late years that the historical development of linguistic forms begins to be illustrated in methodical collections from the later documents.[1]

And much still remains to be done here. It would, for instance, be of the greatest interest for the investigation which I am attempting here if there existed a competent and reasonably exhaustive discussion of the loanwords from French and Middle English in the medieval period. It is uncertain, perhaps it will always remain uncertain, whether these borrowings in a given case are from the French, or mediately from previous English loans from the French. If we could safely distinguish here, it would be a simpler

[1] The lamented death of J. Strachan deprived us of a Middle-Irish Grammar, preliminary studies for which he had published in the Journal of the Philological Society and elsewhere. But valuable work by Sommerfelt, Bergin, Miss Knott, T. F. O'Rahilly, and others encourages us to hope that the main lines of the literary speech of the Middle Ages will be determined within a measurable period.

matter to determine the immediate sources of certain translated texts.

Another class of investigator sometimes attracted to Irish is the anthropologist, the comparative religionist, and that type of student whom I have seen described in an American context as a storyologist. These are all studies of recent development, and the more pedestrian investigator of a particular field is sometimes affected by a mixed feeling of resentment and something like envious admiration as he watches their confident invasion of his province. I do not see how they can be denied a right of entry, and in any case they would take it, but it is always well to remember that a man who claims for his subject all the centuries of recorded and unrecorded history and sometimes the whole range of inhabited space is liable to misinterpret details of some particular place and time which to the stay-at-home student have quite another bearing and relevance. These students too are naturally drawn to the oldest records and to real or supposed survivals of ancient traditions in the later texts. But, until the whole literature has been thoroughly sifted, it is often difficult to determine what is of old tradition, what of recent invention—for men do sometimes invent out of their own heads—or combination, and what is borrowing or adaptation from another tradition. It is always well, in a given instance, to inquire whether the facts can be explained from the conditions of the particular literature in its own environment reinforced by more immediate influences before we have recourse to these more general explanations. And, until the medieval period, which handed on and modified the older Irish tradition, has been thoroughly studied, we cannot fully understand those conditions or determine the exact bearing of the appearance of a universal theme in an Irish dress.

Another and even more insidious enemy of our subject is the popular and general use of the word 'Celtic' in literary criticism. Irish literature may be properly described as 'Celtic', if we are to understand by that simply that it is the product of a people speaking a Celtic language. But the word is commonly taken to mean much more than that, and calls up at once in the mind a whole complex of characteristics that carries with it an almost irresistible suggestion. This is a quite recent development of significance, fortunately unknown, as the word itself was, to the writers of Irish literature throughout its long history. Indeed it has been claimed by Professor Eoin Mac Neill that the revived use of the classical word 'Celtic' is to be dated from the time of the Scotch scholar, George Buchanan, in the late sixteenth century. And modern conceptions of Celtic literature derive their origin from the beginnings of the romantic movement in the middle of the eighteenth century. Thomas Gray invented the Bard, and there could be nothing less like the poet of the Irish, or the Welsh, Middle Ages than the mystic suicide of his famous ode. Macpherson's Ossian filled in the details, and since his time vagueness and mist and an indefinite use of dubiously poetic language has been generally held to be the indubitable mark of Celticism.

In modern time Irish tradition (read in translations) has been taken as the subject matter of a new literature, largely poetical and not unjustly described as Neo-Celtic, which has imported a latter-day mysticism into the handling of the old matter. There can, I think, be no reasonable objection to this process. It is a poet's business to take his good where he finds it and to make the best of it, and he is under no obligation to adopt a strictly historical attitude towards his borrowings. But it is another matter when criticism begins to interpret the past in the light of these modern imaginations, and it is plain that much of the critical writing on Irish and Welsh subjects since the rise of the Romantic school has been dominated by this 'Celtic' prepossession.

The picture of Celtic literature drawn by Ernest Renan and Matthew Arnold—neither of whom, I believe, knew any Celtic language—does not carry any conviction to those who read the original texts in their own setting, for it rests upon an artificial selection of subjects and episodes and, of necessity, can tell us nothing of those subtle and characteristic effects which the peculiar turn and idiom of a language lend to the handling of a subject. For in literature it is not subject that matters, but treatment. And the extreme concreteness of the Irish way of thought is reflected in the idiom of their language and determines the effect of the literature upon any mind which is at all attuned to distinctions of style. There is one characteristic of Celtic speech, for instance, which gets little notice in modern criticism, although it was the first thing to strike the Romans when they came in contact with the Celts. The elder Cato tells us that the Celts were distinguished for their aptitude for fighting and for subtle speech. The Irish have well maintained these two characters. Indeed, I think if one were asked what characteristic was to be found everywhere in Irish literature from the first records down to the tales and popular sayings current among the peasantry to-day, the answer must necessarily be: a sharp and homely brevity of epigrammatic speech eminently calculated for the rapid thrust and return of contentious talk. The concrete cast of language, the epigrammatic concision of speech, the pleasure in sharp, bright colour which we find everywhere in the best of the literature, is confused in the worst periods and examples by strange pedantries of rhetorical expansion, which appear to derive from a native tendency to display, fostered by the influence of the more degenerate kinds of late Latin rhetoric. But these characters, never far away and emerging everywhere whenever nature can get the better of the conventions of the schools, are inherent in the very being of the language as a spoken tongue and cannot be carried over into translation. They are the extreme antithesis of the twilight vagueness which in popular criticism is often associated with the word 'Celtic', and, if any modern literature is inspired by that conception, we shall rightly admire it for qualities of its own, but we may be very sure that those qualities are not Irish, and, as they do not appear to be Welsh either, we shall perhaps be on safer ground if we claim that they are not 'Celtic' at all in any real sense of the word.[1]

It is then perhaps better not to use the word 'Celtic' as an epithet of Irish literature, but to call it simply Irish, begging no ethnological or aesthetic questions and taking up a purely historical attitude. Here again the emphasis has been always laid upon the early literature, for it was natural to look for the pure, uncontaminated Celt in the rich remains of the only literature of Celtic speech which preserved any considerable body of original matter of a date prior to the twelfth century. And indeed it is certain that any Irish claim to have produced one of the most fascinating of the world's literatures must be based upon the works of this early period, whether we consider the pagan epic cycle in which the men and women of the heroic world act violently and crudely and splendidly and speak with a sharp and witty emphasis in an unspoiled world of clear colours and stories; or the poetry of the Christian period, instinct with an unreasoned ecstasy of faith, or speaking of the natural

[1] Mr. H. I. Bell, speaking of the poetry of the Gogynfeirdd, says: 'Neither are they mystical. They have at times that wonderful morning freshness, that sense of a new creation, which gives so much of its peculiar charm to early Celtic poetry, and they are not free from mystification, not only in the affected obscurity of their style, but in the neo-Druidic tendency of which, even so early, there seem to be traces; but this is not mysticism. Even farther from the truth is the idea that Celtic poetry is misty and loves subdued colours. On the contrary, its characteristic is sharp, clear outline, a cloudless atmosphere, a passion for bright, primary colours.' (*Welsh Poems of the Twentieth Century*, 1925, p. 94.) This is true, *mutatis mutandis*, of Irish poetry also.

things and living creatures not as the occasional relaxation of men whose real life is elsewhere, but as the familiar companions and intimate environment of their everyday being.

This time passed without returning, but the later period is not to be neglected because it has not just this interest. The literature goes on and develops new ways of treating the old matter and takes into itself a new matter from without. It is this new matter, the literature of the European world of the time, with which we are here concerned. It will appear that there were means by which external influences could work upon the Irish mind, and that very extensive borrowings were made which blended with, and in many ways modified, the long-descended tradition of the schools.

In the late fifties of the twelfth century, we have seen, the abbot of Terryglass, a monastery of Leinster origin, but on Munster soil where northern Tipperary runs up along the shores of Loch Derg to the Shannon, was writing the quires of the great book which we know as the Book of Leinster, sending it piece by piece as he wrote to the bishop of Kildare for his approval. It is the last gathering of the lore of ancient Ireland: the *Lebor Gabála*, the book of the conquests and the kings; the *Táin Bó Cuailnge* with its attendant cycle of tales; the *Dindshenchas*, in prose and verse, detailing the legends of the famous places; innumerable poems recording the triumphs of the kings of Leinster and other Irish dynasties; the teachings of Cormac and other wisdom texts; and at the end the Martyrology of Tallaght and other religious texts apparently deriving ultimately from the manuscripts of that monastery. This vast *bibliotheca* sums up for us all the learning of the monastic period of Irish manuscript writing. It is noteworthy that it contains only a little of the Ossianic cycle which we have seen was in its developed form the creation of a later age.

Along the top of one of the pages of this book runs a note added a little later:[1]

O Mary! 'tis an ill deed that has been done in Ireland this day, Diarmaid the son of Donnchadh Mac Murchadha, king of Leinster and of the Danes, has been banished oversea by the men of Ireland. Alack! alack! O Lord! what am I to do?

When this note was written the book was still in all probability in the monastery of Terryglass where it had been written. In virtue of the situation of Terryglass, Aed Mac Crimthainn, the writer of the manuscript, was styled professor of learning to the king of Munster, while as successor to Colum mac Crimthainn, the founder of his house, who was of the royal blood of Leinster, he had the title of chief historian of that province. The monk of Terryglass who thus lamented the banishment of his king was inspired by a local patriotism and can have had no inkling of the doom which that fateful action was to bring upon his country. The note was written in August 1166, and in May 1169 the advance guard of the foreign allies whom Diarmaid had summoned to his aid landed at Bannow, three shiploads of mailclad men by whom, say the Four Masters with a bitter irony, the Gaels set little store. The invaders were a mixed host of Welshmen, Flemings, and English captained by Norman *condottieri*. From these leaders, and from others that followed them, there was to develop a new aristocracy in Ireland, those chieftains of the Old English who in the later Middle Ages vied with the native aristocracy in the patronage of Irish historians, brehons, and poets. But before the writing of the Book of Leinster and the invasion from England another movement had been set on foot which in itself marked the end of the monastic period of Irish literature. The previous half-century had seen a systematic reorganization of the Irish Church. The famous

[1] Atkinson, *The Book of Leinster*, introduction, p. 7.

St. Malachi, who had rebuilt Bangor, where the Irish tradition of history began, only to see it destroyed again, founded in 1142 the monastery of Mellifont in the beautiful valley near the Boyne, building it in the pure early Cistercian style which he had admired at Clairvaux, the home of his master St. Bernard. This was the first introduction of the continental Orders into Ireland. The process once begun was naturally accelerated after the English invasion, and in the later Middle Ages the two aristocracies, Gaelic and English, were equally active in the foundation and endowment of monasteries and friaries. As the new houses multiplied and flourished the older foundations decayed. But, just as the new Anglo-Norman lords, ruling over Irish subjects and marrying Irish wives, became in the proverbial phrase, *Hibernis ipsis Hiberniores*, so the new monastic houses, at first stocked with foreign monks, gradually became assimilated to their surroundings, were filled with Irish inmates and adopted Irish speech. This is particularly clear in the case of the Franciscans. The Minorites, first definitely introduced into Ireland in 1231 or 1232, spread rapidly as was their custom, and by 1252 the province was divided into custodies. By 1282 there were four custodies, those of Dublin, Drogheda, Cork, and Nenagh, though later the headship of the custody of Cork seems to have been transferred to Cashel. In the latter part of the thirteenth century racial feeling began to develop, and a letter of Nicholas Cusack, bishop of Kildare, warns Edward I that certain religious of the Irish tongue belonging to different Orders of friars were making trouble.[1] They were holding secret meetings of the native Irish and their princes, and instigating them to rebellion, telling them that they were justified by human and divine law in fighting for their country and attacking the English conquerors, seizing their goods and

---

[1] Fitzmaurice and Little, *Materials for the History of the Franciscan Province of Ireland*, introduction, p. xxii.

appropriating them to themselves. He advises that religious of Irish sympathies should be removed from the convents in dangerous districts and only good and select Englishmen with English companions should be sent among the Irish in future. So also a State Paper of 1285 recommends that no Irishmen should be bishops or archbishops, because they always preach against the king and provide their churches with Irishmen so as to ensure the election of Irishmen as bishops to maintain their language. 'In like manner the Dominicans and Franciscans make much of that language.' The quarrels between the two parties in the Order became fiercer until in the General Chapter at Cork in 1291 they came to blows and a number of friars were killed. The enmity grew so fierce that in the early fourteenth century one Brother Simon declared solemnly that it was not a sin to kill an Irishman and, if he himself did such a deed, he would not on that account refrain from celebrating mass.[1] As a consequence of this indecent enmity an attempt was made to effect a clean separation between the Irish and the English friars and to concentrate the Irish friars in the custody of Nenagh, which included the houses of Nenagh, Athlone, Ennis, Clare Galway, Galway, Armagh, Cavan, and Killeigh. The policy appears to have failed, and the houses in the English part gradually lost importance, while the custody of Nenagh became the real effective centre of the Franciscan Order in Ireland. Dr. Little points out that only in the Franciscan Annals of Nenagh do we find references to lectors and draws the conclusion that 'the intellectual life of the province had among the Irish friars acquired a special importance'.[2]

The conclusion from all this is that in little more than a century the Franciscans in Ireland had followed the general trend of affairs in the island and become Irish in language and sympathies. This change is registered in the literature

[1] Ibid., p. xxiv.　　　　　　　　　　[2] Ibid., p. xxviii.

of the later Middle Ages. It was natural that the recruit-
ment of the monastic Orders should draw largely upon the
families dedicated to literary pursuits. Thus Clarus mac
Maoilín O'Mulconry, a member of the chief family of
historians in Connacht, founded the monastery of the Holy
Trinity in the island of that name in Loch Cé in County
Roscommon in 1215 for Premonstratensian Canons. The
Book of Annals of this house is still in existence, written at
first in an Anglo-Norman hand, but as the annals become
contemporary changing to the Irish script.[1] So the Annals
of Innisfallen in Munster, the earlier portions of which are
written in a magnificent Gaelic script of the late eleventh
century, in the course of the thirteenth century adopt the
new script from abroad, but gradually revert to the native
style or to the curiously mixed form to which Dr. Best gives
the name Anglo-Irish. As with the script, so with the
literature. Partly through the influence of the new religious
orders, partly through the literary interests of the new
Anglo-Norman aristocracy now become Irish-speaking, the
Latin and vernacular literature of medieval Europe gradually forced its way into the closely guarded domain of the
Irish tradition. The continental themes necessarily suffered
a sea-change in the process. One striking example may be
given in proof of this. We have seen that the poetic family
of the O'Dalys claimed that their remote ancestor had
studied his art under Colmán mac Lénine, the poet who
became a monk in the sixth century. In this medieval time
many members of the family imitated the example of the
master of their race. In fifteenth-century manuscripts we
find a life of St. Margaret ascribed to a Philip O'Daly,
Premonstratensian Canon of the house of the Holy Trinity
in Loch Cé, or of its daughter house in Loch Oughter in

---

[1] These Annals are contained in the Cotton MS. Titus A. xxv. For the
evidence connecting them with the house of the Holy Trinity in Loch Cé and
their curious history, see *B.M. Cat.* i. 4 f.

County Cavan. It is a remarkable composition, written in the bardic style with intercalated poems, a religious romance tricked out in all the strange rhetoric of the schools. Other such compositions are frequent in the manuscripts, the poet-monks expending on the new religious themes all the curious devices of an art developed for purposes so strangely different. Another O'Daly of the late fourteenth century, Tadhg Crookshanks was his name in the world, joined the Franciscans and went abroad to study. He has left us a farewell to his country, his friends, and his art which recalls in this later age the emotions of that king of Leinster who was healed by a divine dream of 'a great and sore longing for his fatherland and his children, his kindred and his dear friends'. And here again we meet the same motive for the 'white martyrdom' of pilgrimage, the surrender of all the objects of the natural affections:[1]

For Éire's love I quitted Éire, a poor brother of little learning, hard though it was to leave the green-grassed land of Fál and all the friends I left behind me there. I went from Éire of the kings for love of God, not hate of her, not in wild yearning for a further shore did I quit the companies of Éire. Woe was my heart to leave her coast, though 'twas a holy thing to go into far lands away from my fosterers. I did violence to my heart's desire and passed from among my friends and comrades across the perils of the raging sea. Be it to my good and to theirs that I went from my mother's mother and all her children, though dear that gathered band of friends! Never would I have told them of my going, my comrades and the sharers of my feasts, though good the tale to tell, were it not for an example that I told it. God knows that I repent me that for so long I delayed to leave the great rewards and the honours of Éire to find a better honour. It is not that I repent me to have bidden farewell to Éire and not for the sorrow that pierced me through that I have made these staves. I have heard tell that after the world's way my friends make moan

[1] O'Rahilly, *Measgra Dánta*, 132.

that I have bent under religion's yoke and turned my back upon my comrades. Were I a young lad, sole heir of a great lord yonder in my father's land where I was wont to be, then were it right to grieve for my sake. A child there was whose action was no child's, a king's son and his only heir—Louis the comely, the slender. Into this order of poverty that I have joined he came in his young years—a sorrowful story of another age—the heir of the folk of Sicily. Now when the great news had gone abroad, came the noble-hearted father in quest of his son, and with him a weaponed mailclad host. The graceful-handed, goodly steadfast youth, the lad so holy in his tender years, demanded of his father, master of the host, the reason of that muster. 'It is that I see no son to follow after me but thee, thou countenance of smouldering fire, my darling child; 'tis ill to strive with friends.' 'If thou wilt swear to me,' said the lad, 'O branch of rich bestowing, that after thy death thy inheritance shall surely be mine, I will not go from thee. To abandon God for an unsure inheritance were surely ill-done; speak only of a likely thing and think not so to order this matter. Often the father outlives the son, neither thou nor I can affirm that I shall be thy heir.' The father knew for truth that homily untouched of folly the childlike Louis preached, and the great king's heart was changed within him. 'According to the best that is revealed to thee do thou', said the father to the lad. 'Thy purpose has wrung my heart, my darling, my perfume-breathing branch.'

They parted from one another, the boy and the unblemished chief, the lad in joy, the father with wailing. Said the father to the boy's mother: 'It wilders me whene'er I think that we have neither man nor woman of our seed or succession in all the realm.' The queen of gracious wisdom made answer to her lord: 'For the sorrow of this calamity my heart is a wave of grieving.' Little wonder that they grieved for the king's sole heir, the wand of mighty deed, so splendid is the world. Many a king's self, many a king's son, many a noble's son have turned their back upon the world. Why should any grieve for a poor man, the son of poor folk, what concern to any that clay should cover him or by what way he should die? It is not that I measure myself with that fresh youthful countenance, but 'tis a holy tale that I have told of the brighthaired sweetvoiced noble. For Christ's sake—though I make no boast thereof— have I left the people of the Gael whom I longed to have ever at my hand, and for love of Him have I deserted Éire. For love of Mary and her son have I deserted Éire, for her the twining tress of virgin hair, for Him the shapely branch of golden locks.

The apologue used here to point the moral is entirely characteristic of the time, the place, and the literary and religious milieu. The thirteenth century saw a great development of the collections of *exempla*, or moral stories, which are so marked a feature of the later Middle Ages. These handy collections were the vade-mecums of preachers, and many sermons supply us with examples of their use. From the popular preaching they passed into the popular tradition, and there they still survive to-day, often strikingly divorced from any moral application. The chief medieval collections of the kind were made by the Dominicans, specifically the preaching friars. But the Franciscans also made such compilations, and one such collection, the *Liber Exemplorum*, put together by an English Franciscan living in Ireland about 1275, still survives. From such sources the Irish bards took the tales which they use to point their morals and adorn their poems. The tale in the present case has a peculiar application for a Franciscan bard. It is a curious blend of the exemplary tale found in various collections of the kind: those of Jacques de Vitry and Étienne de Bourbon in the thirteenth, and of the Franciscan Nicole Bozon in the early fourteenth century, with the true story of the entry of the Franciscan saint, Louis of Toulouse, son of Charles II, king of Naples and Sicily, into the Franciscan Order in 1296. The exemplary tale tells how a son, taking on the religious habit, was pursued by his father with an armed force, and told him that he would only return to the world if his father would abrogate the evil custom whereby 'a calf dies as soon as a cow, a son as a father, a boy as an old man'. The application of this tale to the case of St. Louis, and with the necessary modifications to Tadhg Crookshanks O'Daly, is obvious and very happily imagined. From the thirteenth to the seventeenth century such *exempla*, and stories from the native tradition used in the same way, abound in the poetry of the bards, and this is one of the many ways in which the new religious matter reacted on the ancient literature of Ireland.

The other influence, that of the Anglo-Irish aristocrats in touch with continental literature, is steadily on the increase throughout this period. Three vernaculars, Irish, French, and English, were currently spoken over large parts of Ireland in the Middle Ages, although in the battle of tongues the victory inevitably inclined to the Irish side. At the end of the period we find in the library of the ninth Earl of Kildare 34 Latin books, 36 French, 20 Irish, and 22 English. The Fitzgeralds of the east were far more identified with English culture than the families of Norman origin who lived among the Irish of the west. We shall see that the Desmond Fitzgeralds had become assimilated in their attitude to the Irish culture with the native aristocracy, entertaining bards and historians and themselves composing in Irish.

The general literary landscape will now, I hope, be reasonably clear. The various processes which had been at work somewhat obscurely through the first centuries after the invasion from England had, by the end of the fourteenth century, brought about the political and literary situation which was to last until the Tudor time. The sphere of direct English influence was limited to the Pale. In the rest of Ireland Irish was the predominant speech except in the towns, where it was also understood. The linguistic map of Ireland at the end of the period was drawn by Stanihurst in 1577: 'As all the ciuities and towns in Ireland, with

Fingal, the king his land (in the south-west of co. Dublin), Meth, the countie of Kildare, Louth, Weisford, speake to this daie English . . . even so in all other places their natiue language is Irish.' The new nobility of English origin in the west very generally spoke Irish, though those of the south and east were, no doubt, still well acquainted with the French that had been the language of fashion and the English that was replacing it. The houses of the new Orders were becoming entirely Irish in speech and outlook, although here too we must allow for the use of French and English in the south and east. The poets and historians of the older type were busily engaged in reviving and recasting the ancient tradition, as may be plainly seen from the great manuscripts which begin to be written at this time. And in another type of book written by medical scribes or under the influence of the new religious Orders the European literature of the time begins to make its appearance in an Irish dress.

But before considering the kinds of literature and the particular texts which were thus taken over, it will be well to examine the extant manuscripts in the hope of discovering, if we can, the authors and the place of composition of some at least of the texts in question. It will be seen that the manuscripts group themselves naturally in such a way as to suggest conclusions which a consideration of the individual texts serves to confirm.

The chief manuscripts in which the literature with which we are concerned is contained are all of the fifteenth century, and appear to represent the immediate result of the situation just outlined. They were written in the main by scribes of the new type in a district extending from counties Cork and Tipperary through Clare into Roscommon, with an extreme outlier in Donegal. These books also include in some instances texts of the older national tradition borrowed from the books of the older class of hereditary historians, and matter of the new kind sometimes strays into those other books, but on the whole the distinction between the two kinds is clearly marked. This new literature of translation and adaptation is written in an Irish which has shed its archaic characters and already approximates to what we know as the modern language. The aim of the translators was to serve a practical need, whether physical as in the case of the medical texts, or spiritual as in the devotional. And so they appear to have used the ordinary language of the time with an ease and freedom which is very much lacking in their contemporary historians and poets. These texts have been little explored for grammatical and lexicographical purposes, but there is no doubt that much is to be learnt from them of the greatest value for the early history of the modern language. It is therefore the more desirable to date and localize them so far as the material allows, and I shall hope to make some suggestions contributory to that end.

Of manuscripts of this class some fourteen or fifteen are known to me either by personal inspection or by adequate description. There are probably others in existence, but an account based upon the evidence of this particular group will probably hold true in general terms for any others that may be discovered. Here, too, as with all Irish manuscripts, we may be sure that we have only a fragment of what once existed, but I incline to think that this surviving remnant will afford a sufficient basis for at any rate a general picture.

Perhaps the most interesting manuscript for our immediate purpose is that classed as F. 5. 3 in the library of Trinity College, Dublin.[1] It was written about 1454, apparently in a Franciscan house in Clare, and contains

[1] A full description of this manuscript would be interesting, both from the point of view of Irish medieval literature and of Franciscan scholarship in Ireland. A brief notice of both the Latin and Irish portions is in T. K. Abbott, *Cat. of MSS. in T.C.D.*, 1900, under nos. 667, 1699, and a fuller account of the Irish part alone is in Abbott and Gwynn, *Cat. of Irish MSS. in T.C.D.*, 1921, p. 323.

matter in Latin and Irish and even a fragment in English. The Latin texts are in many cases the originals of the Irish versions found in the group under consideration, and the Irish part includes renderings of these and of other related literature. An Irish manuscript, written not much later in County Roscommon, the Liber Flavus Fergusiorum,[1] has the most representative collection of matter common to the group, and gives us the names of some of the translators, all of whom belong to this western area. Other manuscripts of this kind are the Royal Irish Academy MS. 24 P. 25, which, though written in Donegal, is intimately related to the Liber Flavus, and British Museum, Egerton MS. 1781, written in the second half of the century in Donegal and County Cavan.[2] These books were all written for chiefs of the older Irish families. But a second division of the group shows us that the Anglo-Irish nobility, now thoroughly acclimatized, shared the same tastes and patronized the scribes of Irish books. The British Museum Additional MSS. 11809 and 30512, and three Irish manuscripts at Oxford, Paris, and Rennes, take us into another region of scribal activity, the Munster counties of Cork and Tipperary. The Oxford MS. Laud Misc. 610 was written about 1454, in part at any rate, by a member of one of the old scribal families, Seán buidhe O'Clery, for an Anglo-Irish noble, Edmond son of Richard Butler.[3] The Additional MS. 30512 was perhaps written about the same time by a medical scribe, William Mac an Lega, one of the most

---

[1] For the Liber Flavus Fergusiorum see the description by E. Gwynn, *Proc. Roy. Irish Acad.* xxvi. 6, pp. 15–41.

[2] For 24 P. 25 see P. Walsh, *Leabhar Chlainne Suibhne*, Introduction, and for Egerton 1781 see the *B.M. Cat.* ii. 526–45.

[3] For Add. 11809 see the *B.M. Cat.* ii. 545–51. Add. 30512 is described, ibid. 470–505. The Oxford MS. Laud. Misc. 610 is described by J. H. Todd, 'Account of an ancient Irish MS. in the Bodleian Library', *R.I.A. Proc.* ii. 336–45, the Paris MS. Celt. I in Omont's 'Catalogue des MSS. Celtiques . . . de la Bibl. Nat.', *Rev. Celtique*, xi. 389, and the Rennes MS. in ibid. xv. 79–91 (by G. Dottin).

prolific scribes of the fifteenth century. Both books contain, in addition to the literature we are concerned with here, a great deal of matter of old tradition, secular and ecclesiastical. The MS. 11809 was written by this same Mac an Lega, and was discovered in the nineteenth century hidden in the wall of Hoar Abbey in Cashel, County Tipperary. Mac an Lega also wrote a considerable part of the Paris MS. Celt. I, apparently for the MacCarthys. And the Rennes manuscript seems to have been written for the Franciscan house of Kilcrea near Bandon, County Cork. These manuscripts contain many of the texts found in the northern group, and it is clear that there was a considerable interchange of literature between the two districts. A consideration of two different texts will attest this intercourse. The Life of St. Margaret, which, as we shall presently see, was in all probability composed in the north of Roscommon, appears in the Laud MS. written in the east of County Tipperary. And an even more definite instance is the Irish version of Mandeville's travels, which, translated in the south of County Cork by Fínghin Ó Mathghamhna in 1475, was copied into Egerton 1781 in County Cavan in 1484.

The literary men of medieval Ireland were no stay-at-homes, they passed readily from the house of one chieftain to another, from monastery to monastery, and appear to have both spoken and written one literary dialect. This is true even of Scotland, which through the whole medieval period was in literary matters entirely under Irish domination. Some of our texts are found in manuscripts apparently written by Scottish scribes in Ireland, and the books of Scotch leeches contain tractates translated by Irish physicians. These books, it will be noticed, were commonly written for the use of the nobility, whether of Irish or English origin, and imply a reasonable amount of literary culture in those patrons who also shared in the movement by the composition of Irish prose and verse. And we shall expect to find the influence of all these various classes—the old and new nobility, the old and new scribes, the religious of the new Orders, and the traditional poets—reflected in the literature of the fifteenth century.

The religious literature of Latin origin which preponderates in these volumes may be taken first. The centuries between the fourteenth and the seventeenth are in Ireland the Franciscan centuries. And I think it may be claimed that the Irish were naturally Franciscan, Franciscan before St. Francis. For, when we read the records of the early Church, the legends, the poems, the rules, we cannot escape the feeling that we are here in presence of a rehearsal of the Franciscan drama, centuries before it was first staged at Assisi. For where they are most characteristic and least dulled by later unimaginative repetition, these records have that very air of morning freshness which surrounds the early Franciscan traditions. In that young experience the world is born anew and the dews of that rebirth keep miraculously fresh every action and every utterance of the saints. In their poetry all natural things and creatures are seen as with an eye made magically clear and simple by some strange chastity of vision. And this faculty they had conquered for themselves, as the Franciscans were to do later, by extreme austerity.

It has appeared that the manuscript which reveals to us the Latin sources on which the translation literature drew is of Franciscan origin. And the nature of many of the texts, even where the originals are not of immediate Franciscan authorship, betrays that peculiar character which the new missionary Order communicated to European literature in the later Middle Ages. This character, the insistence upon a kind of direct personal share in the agony of the Passion of Christ, symbolized in St. Francis's acceptance of the stigmata, is most vividly seen in those poems which represent the Virgin as in a manner the living concentration of all the sorrow of humanity in the immediate presence of the Crucifixion. The famous Franciscan hymn 'Stabat mater dolorosa' is the example and type of all this poetry, which develops into a particular kind, the 'Planctus', or 'Complaint'. It is interesting to observe that the literature from which most of the commonplaces of this kind of poetry were drawn is well represented in the translations of our period.[1]

Thus the Meditations on the Life of Christ, at this time apparently without good reason attributed to St. Bonaventura, was clearly very popular in the Irish version. Several fifteenth-century manuscripts of our group contain the text, and it continued to be copied in Ireland down to the nineteenth century. In the late seventeenth century a poem on the Life of Christ was based on this text. The Passion section, here as elsewhere, was copied separately for the purpose of devotional meditation. This translation, like so much of the literature we are here considering, was made in Connaught, for it is recorded in a manuscript of 1461 that the author was Tomás Ó Bruacháin, a canon of Killala cathedral in Mayo.[2] Two other texts, one and perhaps both of which belong to Connaught, are of the same tradition. One of these, the Dialogus de passione Christi,

[1] For the commonplaces on the passion cf. Egerton MS. 1781, f. 38, and Rennes MS., f. 31 b; and for a homily on the Virgin see Add. 30512, f. 103; Add. 11809, f. 37; Rennes MS., f. 25; Rawl. B. 513, f. 5. See also the tract partly based on the section 'Maria' in the Manipulus Florum of Johannes Wallensis and Thomas de Hibernia, in Add. 30512, f. 98 b; Rawl. B. 512, f. 145; Rawl. B. 513, f. 3 b; Paris MS., f. 38; Rennes MS., f. 22.

[2] The manuscript of the version of pseudo-Bonaventura which gives the translator's name is R.I.A. MS. 23 B. 3. In another copy (T.C.D. E. 3. 29, no. 1434) it is associated, as in Add. 11809, with the version of the Vita Rhythmica attributed to 'Germanus historiographus' mentioned below. The passion section appears separately as 'Friday's portion' in Egerton 136, art. 26 (*B.M. Cat.* ii. 562). The poem on the life of Christ appears in Egerton 179 (*B.M. Cat.* ii. 40) and T.C.D. H. 4. 11. For the whole subject see *B.M. Cat.* ii. 546–8. It may be of interest to call attention here to the latest study of the question of the authorship, &c., of the original Latin Meditationes by P. Livario Oliger, 'Le Meditationes Vitae Christi', *Studi Franciscani*, Arezzo, Anni vii, viii.

attributed wrongly to St. Anselm, was translated by Seán Ó Conchubhair, probably the Roscommon man of that name who died in 1405. The other, St. Bernard's Book of the Passion of Christ and of the sorrows and complaints of His mother, if indeed it be St. Bernard's, seems to have been translated at the same time and perhaps by the same man. Both of these are found in the Liber Flavus and in other manuscripts of the group.[1] Other collections of common-places on the Passion and the Virgin, drawn largely from the writings of St. Bernard, supply material to the poets when they dedicate their art to religious ends.[2] The poetry of this movement is best represented in the published texts by the works of Angus O'Daly, known as Aonghus na Diadhachta, edited by Father Lambert McKenna. There is one strange and characteristic conception found repeat-edly in his verse which I find hard to parallel from medieval literature, though I think it can be found implicit in the art of the time. This is a peculiar way of emphasizing the character of the Virgin as the especial representative of humanity before God. Christ in judgement is depicted as showing the wounds received in the Passion and claiming vengeance on mankind for his sufferings. The poet calls on the Virgin to intercede with her son for her human kindred in the character of a nursing mother. I have sometimes thought that this conception may be traced to the repre-sentation of the Last Judgement found before the Penitential Psalms in fifteenth-century Books of Hours, which can be carried back at least as far as the thirteenth century. Thus in the British Museum Additional MS. 38116 in a repre-

[1] The version of the Liber de Passione Christi is in the Liber Flavus, ii, f. 10, and there are other copies in R.I.A. MS. 24 P. 25, p. 110, and Eg. 136, f. 89 b (this manuscript, though written in 1630, obviously derives ultimately from a manuscript or manuscripts of this fifteenth-century period). For the Dialogus of St. Anselm see Liber Flavus, ii, f. 6 b; Laud Misc. 610, f. 15; T.C.D. H. 2. 17, p. 99; H. 4. 22, p. 232.

[2] For these commonplaces see p. 126, note 1.

sentation of the Judgement Christ is depicted as showing his wounds, and the Virgin kneels at the side showing her breast, while, beneath, the souls are separated by angels and devils for bliss or bale. In the Books of Hours such representations are followed by the opening words of the first of the nine Penitential Psalms, 'Domine ne in furore tuo arguas me'. The whole idea of these Irish poems is present here, and it may well be that there is some Latin poem unknown to me expressing this conception, which served as a source for the poet or for the literature on which he drew.

Most of these Passion texts were undoubtedly translated from Latin originals, but we can sometimes prove a Middle English source. Thus a curious tract on the Charter of Peace, in which the body of the crucified Christ is identified in an elaborate metaphor with the instrument between God and man, is translated from a well-known Middle English poem. The exact relation of a poem by Tadhg óg O Huiginn, one of the best-known poets of the fifteenth century on this theme, to the Irish prose text and the various forms of the English poem has not yet been established.[1]

Other translations found in this group of manuscripts come under the heading of affective or ascetic theology. Several works by, or in that day attributed to, St. Bonaventura occur, chief among them the Stimulus Amoris, the Pricke of Love, a tract always in favour with the European translators of the time.[2] Other works, like the De miseria conditionis humanae of Innocent III,[3] the pseudo-Augustinian Speculum Peccatoris,[4] and the Liber Scintillarum of Defensor of Ligugé[5] are full of the commonplaces which

---

[1] See *B.M. Cat.* ii. 549. The poem by Tadhg óg Ó Huiginn is in the Yellow Book of Lecan, col. 133ª31.

[2] See *B.M. Cat.* ii. 550.

[3] Geary, *An Irish Version of Innocent III's De Contemptu Mundi*, Washington, 1931.

[4] Paris MS. f. 9; R.I.A. 23 N. 15, p. 59, 23 B. 23, p. 30.

[5] *B.M. Cat.* ii. 549.

made so much of the stuff of private meditation and public exhortation in these late medieval centuries. The work of Innocent III was translated by a certain William Magawney of County Leitrim, the easternmost district of Connaught, as he lay sick of a sword-wound and had ample leisure to consider the misery of the human state. A little group of texts on confession and the sacraments, which remind one of the priest's manuals of the time, no doubt had a more immediately practical end.[1] One, perhaps more, of these texts was translated by that same Roscommon man, Seán Ó Conchubhair, whom we have seen as the translator of one or both of the Passion texts dealt with above. All this literature was immediately practical, and we find nothing of the exalted passion of personal mysticism or of the nice quibbling of dogmatic theology. The few scholastic tracts translated by the doctors clearly had no circulation or influence outside of their manuscripts.[2]

The versions of the lives of the popular saints of the later Middle Ages no doubt served a similar end of private reading and pulpit exhortation. They are taken as a rule from the Golden Legend of Jacobus de Voragine or from such lives as we find gathered together in the Sanctuarium of Mombritius. But they often show a striking independence, and the more popular among them tend to appear in different versions. Thus the life of Alexius, who is as pallid an example of male virtue as Patient Grisel is of female, proves its popularity here as elsewhere by appearing in at least three versions.[3] The life of St. Mary of Egypt occurs in the Liber Flavus in the Golden Legend form, and in Add. 30512 in the shape of a poetic romance derived possibly through an English intermediary from an Anglo-Norman poem.[4] Philip O'Daly of the Holy Trinity in Loch Cé,

---

[1] Ibid. ii. 532.
[2] See Shaw, *Féilsgríbhinn Eoin Mhic Néill*, pp. 144–57.
[3] *B.M. Cat.* ii. 530. [4] Freeman, *Études Celtiques*, i. 78.

K

a poet turned Premonstratensian canon, remembering his ancient profession, turns the passion of St. Margaret into a cante-fable of the approved Irish type, and other texts have their style improved out of all reason by the lavish addition of alliterating adjectives. The only known authors of this type of composition are this Premonstratensian O'Daly and the Augustinian, Augustin Mag Raidhin, author of the life of St. John the Divine, both Roscommon men.[1]

More interesting than these are certain texts deriving from the literature of New Testament Apocrypha or dealing with visions of another world. Of the former type is a version of the well-known rhythmical life of the Virgin in Latin verse composed in Germany in the thirteenth century.[2] Of greater interest is an account of the Assumption, based on a very ancient tradition not elsewhere represented in Western literature. This is found in Latin in the Trinity College MS. and in Irish in the Liber Flavus and Laud 610.[3] Another text on the Harrowing of Hell, unparalleled elsewhere, appears to derive from a lost Middle English poem on the subject, and makes a singular and fascinating drama out of a theme which has always provoked dramatic treatment.[4] The Vision of St. Paul appears in Latin in the Trinity MS. and in Irish in the Liber Flavus.[5] The popular story of the Ghost of Guy, which reads like an account of a sitting of a medieval Society for Psychical Research, appears in Latin and Irish in the same two manuscripts. This text is of Dominican origin, but here occurs in a Franciscan setting.[6]

These two Orders of friars, devoted from their beginning to popular preaching, were accustomed to hold the wandering attention of their congregations by the introduction of

---

[1] *B.M. Cat.* ii. 531.   [2] Ibid. 548.
[3] Donahue, *The Testament of Mary*; see also Seymour, *Journ. Theol. Studies*, xxiii. 36.   [4] *B.M. Cat.* ii. 498.
[5] Seymour, *Journ. Theol. Studies*, xxiv. 54.
[6] Mulchrone, *Lia Fáil*, i. 131.

illustrative anecdotes drawn from a strange variety of sources. These tales were collected together into large compendiums of exempla for the convenience of preachers. Professor Little has printed a book of this kind written in a Franciscan milieu in Ireland.[1] And we find the tales scattered up and down our manuscripts in Irish versions, or used by the poets to enliven both their religious and secular compositions. I have already given an example of this kind in the poem of Tadhg O'Daly, and a very considerable collection of these tales, often showing interesting variants from the current types, might be made from our manuscripts. The Liber Flavus has a tale from the collection of the Cistercian, Caesarius of Heisterbach,[2] and another from the famous Disciplina Clericalis of Petrus Alfonsi, the earliest medieval story-book.[3] There are translations of the tale of Barlaam and Joasaph,[4] which is a variant of the story of the Buddha, and of the Seven Wise Masters, another text of ultimately Indian origin.[5] The Disciplina Clericalis had come the same way, for the twelfth century Spanish Jew who wrote it translated his tales from the Arabic, and they had in many cases reached the Moors through Persia from India.

Many of these tales first propagated by the preaching of the friars have survived into modern folk-lore. An old storyteller in West Kerry once told me a tale of happenings on his remote island which I immediately recognized as one of these anecdotes which the Jew Petrus had heard among the Arabs in the twelfth century. It had wandered all the way from India to this westernmost of all European land, possibly assisted in its migrations by the fact that it is a rather improper tale. For these preachers often gave a moral application to themes very ill-suited to the purpose.[6]

[1] See British Soc. of Franciscan Studies, Publications, I, *Liber Exemplorum ad usum predicantium.*

[2] Gwynn, *Ériu,* ii. 82.   [3] *R.I.A. MSS. Cat.* p. 1259.

[4] *B.M. Cat.* ii. 559.   [5] Greene, *Béaloideas,* xiv. 219.

[6] *Disciplina Clericalis,* ed. Hilka and Soderhjelm, p. 15.

We have seen that the books of this religious literature were copied indifferently for the nobles of the old Irish stock and the new Anglo-Norman lords. And representatives of these two classes took their share in the work. The travels of that mendacious knight, Sir John Mandeville, whom we now know to have been a physician of Liége, were translated by an Irish chieftain, Fínghin Ó Mathghamhna.[1] This and the Book of Marco Polo[2] and the letter of Prester John[3] were no doubt turned into Irish to satisfy the interest in Oriental things aroused by the practice of pilgrimage to Palestine. The nobles of Norman descent also practised Irish verse, the art of which they acquired from their attendant poets. A manuscript of the mid-fifteenth century in the British Museum, Additional 30512, sheds a vivid light on the relations of the Tipperary Butlers and the Desmond Fitzgeralds with Irish men of letters. The book was written before 1462 by William Mac an Lega, one of the most prolific scribes of his day, probably for Edmond, son of Richard Butler. The writer of the manuscript provides us with an instance of a new class of scribe which had been actively at work from the fourteenth century onwards. These were the doctors who translated the Latin books of Arabian medicine current in the Middle Ages. They probably found their Latin originals in the new monasteries and in the castles of the Anglo-Norman nobility, but they did not limit themselves to their medical texts and their manuscripts are full of a strangely mixed matter; the new literature of religion, scholastic philosophy, and all the miscellaneous prose and poetry of the Irish tradition. Mac an Lega's book is typical of this other side of the activity of the doctor scribes. The first half of the manuscript is devoted in the main to the literature in prose

---

[1] Stokes, *ZCP.* ii. 1–63, 226–312, 603–4.
[2] Ibid. i. 245–73, 362–438, 603; cf. ii. 222.
[3] *B.M. Cat.* ii. 543.

and poetry of pre-twelfth-century Ireland, while the latter half contains prose only, chiefly of the fourteenth–fifteenth-century period, translated from the Latin, and in two cases possibly from English originals.[1]

Another manuscript written for this same Edmond, son of Richard Butler, still exists. This book, now Bodleian MS. Laud Misc. 610, was written about 1454, mainly by Seán Buidhe O'Clery, a member of the most famous of the Irish historical families. It was named the Psalter, because a considerable portion of its contents derived from the Psalter of Cashel, a famous manuscript originally compiled under the direction of Cormac mac Cuilennáin, king-bishop of Cashel in the ninth century, and supplemented for Brian Bóroma at the end of the tenth or beginning of the eleventh century. In 1462 these two manuscripts were taken in ransom for Edmond Butler by Thomas Fitz-gerald, eighth earl of Desmond, and in the first half of the sixteenth century certain members of the O'Mulconry family retouched faded passages in the manuscript and added a number of texts, some of which deal with the history of the Fitzgeralds, for Maurice, tenth earl of Des-mond, in his house at Askeaton. Later still in the sixteenth century the manuscript would appear to have come back into Butler hands, for a number of poems composed by a Richard Butler of the Kilkenny family are written into

---

[1] For these medical scribes see the Introduction to Miss Wulff's edition of the Irish version of John of Gaddesden's *Rosa Anglica*, and compare Sir Norman Moore's *History of the Study of Medicine in the British Isles*, 1908, and his 'Essay on the History of Medicine in Ireland', *St. Bartholomew's Hospital Reports*, xi. 145–66. The classical account of actual Irish medical manu-scripts is that by S. H. O'Grady in the *B.M. Cat.* i. 171–327. This may be supplemented by Professor Mackinnon's descriptions, *Catalogue of Gaelic MSS. in Scotland*, 1912, 5–71. For the often long and interesting historical notes written by the scribes of medical manuscripts, see an article by P. Walsh, *Irish Ecclesiastical Record*, xx (1922), 113; xxi (1923), 238. A curious instance of an Irish medical scribe working in England is in Trinity College, Cambridge, MS. no. 918.

blank spaces in the book. These poems are religious in subject, and one of them may well be quoted as an example at once of the practice of Irish verse by the hibernicized English, and as a proof of the penetration of the Franciscan attitude, which so profoundly modified the religious poetry of Europe in the later Middle Ages, into the Irish tradition. A note by the scribe of the manuscript states that 'Richard Butler composed this on the day he died':[1]

> Jesu fairer than earth's fairest,
> Thou than lily-blooms more holy,
> Mary's winsome blossom, carest
> But to join thy kindred lowly.

[1] There is nothing in the manuscript to identify this Richard Butler, but one is tempted to associate him with a man of the name mentioned in a letter of William Sayntloo to Cromwell, 17 March 1537, who lived in the 'fasaghe of Banauntry, parcel of the said liberty [of Wexford], let to farm by the King's commissioners, as Mr. Sentleger and others, to Mr. Richard Butler, where inhabiteth Kavenaghes, McMorghowes, judges, and Irish rymers' (*Cal. of Carew MSS.*, 1515–74, p. 116).

Richard Butler's poem, with others by the same author, is in Add. 30512, arts. 90, 94, 98, 101, 114 (h). These beautiful verses may be given here, with a few suggested readings in square brackets where the manuscript is defective.

> Is áille Ísa iná 'n cruinne
> is ná bláth róis nó lile;
> is tú a bláth caomh ó Mhuire
> dochua a ghnáthghae[l] rinne.

> Is millsi iná siúcra
> is ná drucht meala m[? uine]
> is ná mil bríghach bethi
> Ísa mór mac Muire.

> Gidhbé gráidhis Ísa
> na c[h]roidhi go cluthair,
> ní théid [aen] grádh ele
> ann gu dere in domhain.

> Roisderd Buitillér in lá adbath .cc.

> A Ísa mór milis
> a Ísa mac Muire
> dodelbaigh gach inis
> gach mínmhuigh gach muine.

Sweeter than what else is sweetest,
Than sweet dews that fall from Heaven,
Mary's son that earth completest,
Sweeter than bee's honey even.

Whoso longs for Jesu only
In his secret heart concealing,
To the world's end is not lonely,
Through that heart no new love stealing.

Jesu thou hast made for ever,
Sweetest son of Mary maiden,
Every isle in every river,
Every forest tree fruit-laden.

We feel in this poem that subtle interpenetration of human and divine love which is the most marked feature of the religious lyric of the later Middle Ages. It is therefore without surprise that we find the companion art of love-poetry practised at this time. And there is evidence that it owed its introduction into Irish to these same Anglo-Norman aristocrats to whom the two worlds of French and Irish poetry were equally known.

When we turn to themes of a romantic nature we find that some of the same background has to be presupposed. Romance in the Middle Ages was, we know, classified into three matters, the matter of Britain, the matter of Rome, and the matter of France. All three are represented in medieval Ireland. For the matter of Britain it has long been recognized that the themes found in the later romances find at least their analogues, in many cases perhaps their ultimate originals, in the old Irish epic tales. The Arthurian tales of the later type came into Ireland in our period probably through the interest of the Norman nobility in these stories of chivalry. Unfortunately the considerable fragments of texts of this kind in Oxford and Dublin have not found their editor. Some remnants of a Grail story have been printed by Professor Robinson of Harvard, but until the whole material is made accessible it would be premature to make any attempt to define the relation of these Irish versions to the romances in other tongues. It is clear that texts of an unusual kind were current in Ireland, and it may be that interesting discoveries are to be made here. A recent publication of a tale entitled 'The Adventures of the Great Fool', probably of late composition not earlier than the seventeenth century, may serve as an instance of the way in which different themes were combined, probably by the Irish writer. This variation on the theme of the Oaf-knight begins with a passage clearly based on some text of Percival le Gallois and concludes with an adaptation of the temptation motive found in Gawayne and the Green Knight. Gawain appears again in the 'Adventures of the Crop-eared Dog', a kind of werewolf story obviously connected with the tales studied by Professor Kittredge in his *Arthur and Gorlagon*. Another sixteenth-century story shows us how some of these foreign matters came into Ireland. It is called the Adventures of Eagle Boy, and is based on the theme of a child carried away by an animal and returning in manhood to save his wronged mother, the theme of Guillaume de Palerne and other romances. This story the author tells us he based upon a tale told him by a gentleman who had himself heard it told in French. Another French tale of the same type, Florent et Octavian, is also found in Irish. In all these tales episodes drawn from the native tradition are inserted, and the later versions of the older Irish tales borrow again from their French rivals. It is therefore necessary to exercise some caution in using these late versions to reconstruct the pure native tradition, and the possibility of French influence must always be allowed for.[1]

---

[1] For all these classical and medieval texts see R. I. Best, *Bibliography of Irish Philology and of Printed Irish Literature*, 123–6; *Bibliography of Irish Philology and Manuscript Literature* (1913–41), 90–1. The text of the Adven-

The matter of Rome, the romance of antiquity, had been turned into Irish before our period, at the end of the late Middle Irish time. Excellent versions of the tale of Troy, the *Aeneid*, Lucan's *Pharsalia*, and Statius' *Thebaid* were made towards the end of the twelfth century, just at the period when this very matter was coming into French romance. These are the characteristically medieval classics, and the Irish dealt with them in the medieval way, rendering and adapting them with a perfect freedom in a style which had been first developed in the later recensions of their own epic tales. The story of Alexander had come into Irish as early as it came into Anglo-Saxon literature, but it was re-adapted at a later time. There is also a very strange rendering of the story of Ulysses, not paralleled elsewhere so far as my knowledge goes. These texts were all current in our period and exercised a great influence on both its prose and poetry. Thus the fourteenth-century history of the wars in Clare, the Triumphs of Turlough, is deliberately imitated after the Irish Pharsalia, and that internecine conflict is in consequence called by its historian the *bellum civile*. And the names of the classic heroes are frequent on the lips of the bardic poets, who propose their example to the chiefs they celebrate almost as often as the example of Conor and Cuchulainn and the heroes of the Red Branch.[1]

The matter of France is, naturally, less fully represented. Only the Charlemagne cycle is known, and that not in its characteristic forms. This came apparently through the Franciscans in a Latin shape. The Trinity·MS. to which I

tures of the Great Fool is printed by T. Ó Rabhartaigh in *Lia Fáil*, i. 194, and the subject is discussed by L. Mühlhausen in *ZCP*. xvii. 1 ff. For Eachtra an Mhadra Mhaoil see *B.M. Cat.* ii. 271, and for Eachtra Mhacaoimh an Iolair see ibid. 353.

[1] For the matter of Rome see Best as above. Dottin has studied 'La Légende de la Prise de Troie en Irlande', *Rev. Celtique*, xli. 149. For the Irish Alexander cf. Best, p. 124. The *Merugud Uilix maicc Leirtis*, the Irish Odyssey, was separately published by K. Meyer, 1886.

have so often referred contains two of these Latin romances. One is the universally known Chronicle of the Pseudo-Turpin. But the other is a curious and unique Latin version of the chanson of Fierabras. Both of these were translated into Irish and appear in Egerton 1781 and other manuscripts of our group.[1]

These tales then came into Ireland through Latin and French. But the possibility of English originals in some cases must be admitted. Professor Robinson has shown that the characteristically English traditions of Guy of Warwick and Bevis of Southampton appear in Irish at this period in forms which presuppose English originals, and in the case of Guy of Warwick a particular form of the story which has no representative in surviving English manuscripts.[2] And all this literature introduced whether from Latin, French, or English through the interest of the Anglo-Norman nobility or the religious was readily given an Irish colouring and immediately influenced that older tradition of native origin. This influence appears in the new adaptations and new inventions of the tale-tellers, and in the fresh matter found in the religious and secular compositions of the poets.

It was a new treatment of love that came into Ireland in the fourteenth century. In the earlier literature the passions are treated with the seriousness of the heroic age. Deirdre has nothing of the romantic air that some modern representations have given her. She is direct and dangerous and devastating like a storm. And the loves of the heroines of the old sagas are like swift and terrible visitations, speaking in sudden cries and violent actions, never played with or sophisticated or analysed in the romantic fashion. There is beauty enough in the brief descriptions and rapid touches of the old poets, but it is never that cultivated beauty induced by the cool examination of a sentiment under

[1] For the pseudo-Turpin and Fierabras see *B.M. Cat.* ii. 527–9.
[2] For Guy of Warwick and Bevis see *ZCP.* vi. 9–104, 273–338, 556.

different lights and in shifting moods. The men who made the sagas for us had an exquisite sensitiveness to external impressions and they possessed that Celtic art of isolating and defining those impressions in brief and decisive sentences which in the last analysis gives their abiding charm to the best of the Welsh and Irish writings. Consider this episode from the Táin Bó Fraích, a tale perhaps of the eighth century. Meadhbh and Ailill have induced Fraoch, son of a fairy woman and the lover of their daughter Findabhair, to swim in a monster-haunted pool. He is about to leave the water unharmed when Ailill bids him back:[1]

'Come not out of the water,' said Ailill, 'until thou bring me a branch from yonder rowan tree on the river's brink. For its berries are beautiful to me.' Fraoch goes back and breaks a branch from the tree and brings it on his back across the water. And Findabhair cried out: 'Is that not beautiful to see?' For beautiful it was to her to see Fraoch over the dark water, the body so white, the hair so lovely, the face so shapely, the eye of deep grey, and all the tender youth faultless and without blame, his face narrow below and broad above, his straight and flawless make, the branch with the crimson berries between the throat and the white face.

That vision so clearly seen, so surely and swiftly rendered is of the very heart of the saga literature. In the last centuries of the dying Middle Ages and in a mixed culture these instant emotions, these clean certainties are not to be looked for. The first recorded practitioner of this kind is one of the Desmond Fitzgeralds, called Gerald the Rhymer, the first earl, who was Chief Justice of Ireland in 1367 and lived in a close conversation with Irish men of letters. The art of poetry which he learnt from the native tradition he and his fellows applied to the fabrication of little poems in the manner of courtly love, and they make a curious blend

[1] Byrne and Dillon, *Táin Bó Fraích*, § 17.

of the simple-hearted rhetoric of the Irish kind with the sophisticated ironies of society. We shall see in the next chapter the fascinating result of this process and need not dwell upon it here. But I may place here one poem, written late in the period, which makes an original thing out of one of the commonplaces of medieval literature. Love-poetry, when it draws near to reality, must meet at last the inevitable, the final reality of death. And this poetry was itself a product of the dying Middle Ages which everywhere in Europe are marked by an increasing preoccupation with the idea of death. To this period belongs in particular the gruesome theme of the *danse macabre*, where all the classes of mankind, the pope, the emperor, the knight, the lady, the lover are shown stricken suddenly out of life by the menacing lance of the grinning skeleton which stands for the instant terror of death. In Ireland too this conception has its place. A poem, perhaps of the seventeenth century, conveys death's warning to beauty.[1]

> Lovely lady, rein thy will,
> Let my words a warning be,
> Bid thy longing heart be still.
> Wed no man. Remember me.
>
> If my counsel like thee not,
> Winsome beauty, bright of blee,
> Thou know'st not what deeds I've wrought.
> Wed no man. Remember me.
>
> If thou know'st not they are clay:
> That slim form eyes may not see,
> That round breast silk hides away.
> Wed no man. Remember me.
>
> Keep my counsel lest thou slip.
> If love or hate men offer thee,
> Hide thy heart and hoard thy lip.
> Wed no man. Remember me.

[1] O'Rahilly, *Dánta Grádha* (Dublin, 1926), 138.

Wed no man. Remember me.
I shall come thy joy to still,
Though I shall not welcome be.
Lovely lady, rein thy will.

It is little wonder that these poets began to meditate upon death, for already the shadows were creeping across their sky, and the order which had nursed them, and which was the presupposition and the purpose of their being, was already tottering to its fall. This last poem is probably of the seventeenth century, and that century was to see the destruction of all the poets had lived for, the ruin of the patrons on whose bounty they depended, and the obliteration of the ancient landmarks which were all the security they knew.

VI

LOVE'S BITTER-SWEET

THERE is one kind of literature, perhaps the most interesting and certainly the most attractive of all these products of the general European influence, which can with certainty be traced to the originating activity of the Anglo-Norman lords. This is the love-poetry which here as in England develops out of French lyric, but takes a very different form, extremely characteristic of the Irish situation. The subject is love, and not the direct passion of the folk-singers or the high vision of the great poets, but the learned and fantastic love of European tradition, the *amour courtois*, which was first shaped into art for modern Europe in Provence, and found a home in all the languages of Christendom wherever a refined society and the practice of poetry met together. In Irish, too, it is clearly the poetry of society. To prove this, we need only point to the names of some of the authors of the poems: in Ireland, Gerald the Earl, Magnus O'Donnell (the chief of his clan), the earl of Clancarthy, and Pierce Ferriter; in Scotland, the earl and countess of Argyle and Duncan Campbell of Glenorquhy, 'the good knight', who died at Flodden. One is reminded of the company of noble poets, whose love-poems are collected in *Tottell's Miscellany* (1557)—the earl of Surrey, Sir Thomas Wyatt the Elder, and Lord Vaux. The other poets belong to a class which had no representative in England, the bardic order. They correspond in a way to the university men, but their fixed place in society was higher than any that his attainments alone have ever been able to secure for the university man in England. They were, indeed, until the fall of the old Irish order an intellectual aristocracy, with all the privileges and, no doubt, many of the prejudices of a caste. They held their position by virtue of their birth and the practice of their art. It is thus without any surprise that we find them sharing this peculiar art of love-poetry with that other aristocracy of alien conquest or tribal right. And we shall probably not go very far wrong if we hold that just this poetry is the offspring of the marriage of these two orders. In this happy union the aristocrats of position contributed the subject, the aristocrats of art the style. By their intermediation the matter of European love-poetry met the manner of Irish tradition. And in these poems we see how perfect was the fusion, how happy the result.

They inherit the peculiar delight in the details of personal beauty, of flowing hair and slim grace and stately glance, from the eulogistic poetry of the bards. But their inner spirit, though it does not exclude a sincerity of passion, is a subtle preoccupation with the fine points of a realist casuistry of love. The poets profess to be bewildered in a sickness of passion, but they keep their heads surprisingly, and reason like schoolmen on the stages and crises of their complaint, and on the virtues and vices of the infecting cause.

The poems we possess are mostly of a comparatively late date, of the sixteenth and seventeenth centuries. Among the earliest recorded are those preserved in the Scottish Book of the Dean of Lismore of the early sixteenth century. But the tradition and, no doubt, the practice of the art goes back to a much earlier date. We have already met the name of Gerald the Rhymer, fourth earl of Desmond, of that great family of the Fitzgeralds—the 'Greeks' and 'Florentines' of Ireland—which played such a part in the history of Irish literature. He was Lord Chief Justice of Ireland in 1367, and in 1398 he disappeared, says the tale, and sleeps below the waters of Loch Gur, whence he emerges every seven years to ride the ripples of the lake. His wife—she was in history a Butler, Eleanor, daughter of

James, second earl of Ormond—was famed in poetic tradition for her gallantries. It is this romantic figure that stands at the head of our company of poets. Several poems are attributed, rightly or wrongly, to him in the Dean's Book. And the *shanachies* speak of him in their great style:

A nobleman of wonderful bounty, mirth and cheerfulness in conversation, charitable in his deeds, easy of access, a witty and ingenious composer of Irish poetry and a learned and profound chronicler; and, in fine, one of the English nobility that had Irish learning and professors thereof in greatest reverence of all the English of Ireland.

There can be no reasonable doubt that in men such as this our poetry came into being. Acquainted with both worlds, the French world of the matter and the Irish world of the manner, they were admirably placed for introducing this new thing into Irish verse. There are in Harley MS. 913 (fol. 15 b) certain Anglo-Norman verses, which have for a heading 'Proverbia Comitis Desmonie', and these have been attributed to our Gerald. But the manuscript was written before his day. They may serve, however, to prove the practice of French verse in his family. In Irish verse the name of Fitzgerald is famous. In the sixteenth century the eighth earl of Kildare had a fine library of Latin, French, English, and Irish books. In the sixteenth century, too, there was a Fitzgerald, David the Black, who was regarded as a sort of Admirable Crichton. This is what Stanihurst has to say of him:

Dauid Fitzgirald, vsuallie called Dauid Duffe, borne in Kerie, a ciuilian, a maker in Irish, not ignorant of musike, skilfull in physike, a good & generall craftsman much like to Hippias, surpassing all men in the multitude of crafts, who comming on a time to Pisa to the great triumph called Olympicum, ware nothing but such as was of his owne making; his shoes, his pattens, his cloke, his cote, the ring that he did weare, with a signet therein verie perfectlie wrought, were

all made by him. He plaied excellentlie on all kind of instru-
ments, and soong therto his owne verses, which no man could
amend. In all parts of logike, rhetorike, and philosophie he
vanquished all men, and was vanquished of none.

We have none of the poetry of this later Hippias. But
some of the poems of his son, Muiris mac Dháibhí Dhuibh,
are extant, and he plays a part in the *Pairlement Chloinne
Tomáis*, that strange memorial of the contempt of the
bards for the lesser sort. In the eighteenth century Pierce
Fitzgerald of Ballymacoda keeps up the family name for
poetry. And let us not forget here one who, if not a poet, was
a cause that poetry was in others, Mistress Garrett, Surrey's

> 'Fair Geraldine,' a 'Florentine' of this race:
> From Tuskane came my Ladies worthie race:
> Faire Florence was sometyme her auncient seate:
> The Western yle, whose pleasaunt shore dothe face
> Wilde Cambers cliffs, did geue her liuely heate:
> Fostered she was with milke of Irishe brest:
> Her sire an Erle: her dame of prince's blood.

Nor were the Fitzgeralds the only Anglo-Irish family
which patronized and practised Irish verse. Two fifteenth-
century manuscripts, Laud Misc. 610 and Add. 30512,
both belonged alternately to the Fitzgeralds and the
Butlers. And both contain good store of Irish literature of
almost every type and period. The Roches of Fermoy are
honoured in the best bardic style in the Book of Fermoy.
And so we might go on through all the families of the
Gaedheal-Ghoill, establishing for them all a connexion
with Irish poetry. We have already considered the influence of the religious orders, particularly the Franciscans,
who played a great part in the carrying of continental
themes into Irish literature. Brother Michael of Kildare
practised English poetry in the country of the Fitzgeralds.
His poems are found in the same manuscript as the
'Proverbia Comitis Desmonie'.

Certain areas of southern Ireland were indeed, as Professor Curtis has shown us,[1] trilingual in the fourteenth century. Thus Richard Ledrede, bishop of Ossory 1318–60, found that the clerics of his cathedral city were most unclerically fond of singing certain 'base, worldly and theatrical songs' on high days and holidays. These songs were in French and English, and we have examples of them. One English song we immediately recognize as of the type familiar to us in eighteenth-century poetry as *An Seanduine*:

> Alas! hou shold Y syng,
> Yloren is my playing,
> Hou shold Y with that olde man
> To leven and [lose] my leman
> Swettist of al thinge.

The French songs are songs of love of a more popular character than those with which we have to deal here, but related to them in origin.

> Heu alas pour amour
> Qy moy myst en taunt dolour.

So sang the amorous clerics. The learned poet takes up the theme and subtilizes on it in his own manner:[2]

> Love is a sickness and a smart,
> 'Tis idly spoken:
> He will not give me back my heart,
> For it is broken.
>
> O silly heart! to yield to Love
> Yourself deceiving.
> Your case can ne'er my pity move,
> Since mine's the grieving.
>
> Could I but hate who hateth me,
> My freedom proving,
> Since love is naught that I can see,
> Or loved or loving.

---

[1] 'The Spoken Languages of Ireland', *Studies*, viii (1919), 234.
[2] O'Rahilly, *Dánta Grádha*, 71.

Ledrede made the probably vain attempt to substitute sacred songs for these secular lyrics, writing Latin hymns to the same tunes, among which we may recognize interesting and very early examples of Christmas carols. But the damage was already done, and the wanton themes were probably already passing over into Irish to go underground in the popular tradition and to survive and propagate openly in the written verses of the nobles and the poets. For one may suppose that it was through these channels that so many foreign themes came into Ireland. They found there a formed and regulated literature practised by an organized literary class and propagated by academies (if we may so term the bardic schools) conducted on a standardized method. There has never been a country in which the sense of tradition was more intense than in medieval Ireland. Irish literature had been created under the auspices of the Irish church in the period between the sixth and the eleventh centuries. The Norman invaders found this literature established as a part, not only of Irish culture, but also of the tribal organization. It was of the very atmosphere of the people's life, a part of their consciousness as Irishmen, an expression of the forms of their being. The technical devices, imitated originally from Latin sources, had become a necessary part of the equipment of an Irish poet. He thought of literature in these terms, in part by an inevitable predilection, in part as a result of the long and strict training of the bardic schools. The rules of his art were formulated in a series of treatises, the tradition of which begins, at any rate, in the eighth century, and extends to the elaborate summary of the sixteenth century part of which has been edited by Professor Bergin as a Supplement to *Ériu*.[1]

The love-themes, which were now to make their entry into Irish literature, usually carried with them on their pil-

---

[1] Vols. VIII–X and XIV.

grimages certain lyric methods which became acclimatized in all the literatures of Europe. It was not so in Ireland. There the established forms were too strong. It is to be noted that these forms were used for many purposes outside of the more deliberate compositions which are most frequent in our transcripts. Thus already in the ninth century the playful poem of the student and Pangur Bán, his cat, solves easily the problem of putting the *deibhidhe* metre to familiar uses (p. 24 f.). This kind of poetry gets little representation in our manuscripts. But hints here and there—marginal quatrains, stray quotations in commentaries, references in the Annals—show that it persisted in the schools. The presence of the type at a later period is attested by the pleasant poems of sixteenth- to seventeenth-century date printed by Professor Bergin in the *Irish Review*, 1912–13.

These forms, then, were ready to the hand of the adaptors of the new foreign themes. They were the established forms of light and personal verse, and they adapted themselves with ease to the witty turns and delicate dialectic which poetry of this character requires. There has always been in the Irish nature a sharp and astringent irony, a tendency to react against sentiment and mysticism, an occasional bias to regard life under a clear and humorous light. This could easily be illustrated from the older epic tales. Much, indeed, of the exaggeration in those tales—so fiercely ridiculed by certain critics—is the exuberance of a man who sees the fun of the thing, and would not for the world have his monstrosities taken at their face value. And from Mac Con Glinne to Merryman the light of this inexhaustible irony plays upon Irish life and letters. We miss the point of much in the literature if we forget this. Modern mysticism has tended to hide the clear outlines of ancient Irish literature in a veil of mythological fancy and to tempt us to forget the lively humanity lying at the basis of this curious fabric. What with the mythologists, the philosophers, the genealogists, and the topographers, there is a real danger that we may forget the fact that poetry is produced by poets, and that poets are men living in a world of which these honourable sciences can at best give us but an imperfect and partial picture.[1]

> Of women no more evil will I say,
> The lightsome loves that help my heart to live
> —The sun sees nothing sweeter on his way—
> They pledge their faith and break it. I forgive,
> All I forgive and scandal them no more.
> I am their servant. Let the witless jeer.
> Though their slain loves are numbered by the score,
> I love them living and their ghosts are dear.
> The cunning wits are loud in their dispraise,
> And yet I know not. If their breed should fail,
> What comfort were in all the world's wide ways?
> A flowerless earth, a sea without a sail.
> If these were gone that make earth Heaven for men,
> Love them or hate, 'twere little matter then.

This note of light irony is perhaps the master-note of these poems and a chief cause of the fascination they have for us. Here and there, no doubt, one feels a strain of real passion in them—the *odi et amo* of Catullus—*Tugas féin mo ghrádh ar fhuath*. And in these matters the partition that divides the real from the make-believe is notoriously thin. A man may express real feeling through a tradition just as a careless technique need not connote overmastering passion. But, taken in the main, these poets, no doubt, slept none the worse for their love, and died in song to live the more intensely in the foray and the feast. 'Men have died and worms have eaten them, but not for love', says Rosalind, who was a great authority.

[1] O'Rahilly, *Dánta Grádha*, 3.

Here is another example:[1]

> They lie who say that love must be
> A sickness and a misery;
> He that ne'er loved woman knows
> Never anything but woes.
>
> I too love a woman; yet
> My clear eyes are never wet;
> Death has claimed me for his own,
> Yet I live by love alone.
>
> Clad in flesh and blood I move,
> Though a swan-white maid I love;
> Though I love, I eat and sleep,
> Music's service still I keep.
>
> I'm no reed in water swaying,
> My free thought goes lightly playing;
> I'm no lover chill through all
> The piled cloaks of Donegal.
>
> I'm a man like others still,
> Fires burn me, waters chill;
> If the young and strong must die,
> Ne'er so doomed a man as I.
>
> Rope will bind me, this know I,
> Like a sponge my mouth's ne'er dry,
> Softer is my flesh than stone,
> I can't drink the sea alone.
>
> Though love within my bones doth play,
> I know the night is not the day,
> Black's black, white's white, a boat's a boat
> And not a stately ship afloat.
>
> I never call a horse a crow,
> The sea's no hill, that much I know,
> Small is less than great, I feel,
> And a fly smaller than a seal.

[1] O'Rahilly, *Dánta Grádha*, 10.

Though I love her more than all
The sun-riped maids of Donegal,
Yet, by all the gods above!
I'm no sufferer for her love.

Despite his love Cúchonnacht Ó Cléirigh lived to rhyme another day.

There is a delicate sense of beauty, too, in these poems. One notes particularly the delight in the beauty of hair which finds constant expression in the poetry of Ireland in all periods. *Is barr sobarche folt and*—the primrose bloom on the hair is the first in the catalogue of bodily beauties that adorn the people of the Isle of the Blest. And one remembers the hair of Étaín: *Dá triliss órbuidi for a cind ocus fighe chethurdhúaluch for cechtar n-aí ocus mell óir for rinn cech dúail*, 'Two plaits of golden hue upon her head, each plait woven out of four tresses, and a ball of gold upon the end of every tress.' The same hair ripples and shines through these poems, and one of them is an exquisite rhapsody, playing deliciously with words and with the hair that they describe:[1]

Veiled in that light amazing,
Lady, your hair soft-wavèd
Has cast into dispraising
Absalom son of David.

Your golden locks close clinging
Like bird-flocks of strange seeming,
Silent with no sweet singing,
Draw all men into dreaming.

That bright hair idly flowing
Over the keen eyes' brightness,
Like gold rings set with glowing
Jewels of crystal lightness.

[1] Ibid. 17.

> Strange loveliness that lingers
> From lands that hear the Siren;
> No ring enclasps your fingers,
> Gold rings your neck environ.

> Gold chains of hair that cluster
> Round the neck straight and slender,
> Which to that shining muster
> Yields in a sweet surrender.

This might well be the praise of Étaín out of fairy-land.

We have little evidence as to the time of composition of most of these poems. There seems no reason to question the tradition that the few attributed to Earl Gerald are really his, and our conviction here is strengthened by the discovery of a long series of poems by this author in the Book of Fermoy, a fifteenth-century manuscript. And when we read the single example of his work given in *Dánta Grádha*,[1] we see at once that it has nothing to distinguish it in language, sentiment, or expression, from other poems of the kind certainly composed in the seventeenth century at the time of the breaking up of the schools. So that we have the remarkable fact (but in Irish literature it is not remarkable), that poems written at either end of a period of between 300 and 400 years strike upon our ear with the effect of contemporary compositions. This is of course due to the condition of the bardic schools which were a sort of conservative trade union, hedging poetry about with rules and restrictions and jealous of unlicensed innovations. Here is a poem by Niall Mór MacVurich which shows that the tradition lasted in Scotland down to the eighteenth century.[2]

Speech in Silence

> Fie on last night that sped so swiftly by!
> If I must hang, let me be hanged to-night.
> Two in this house are speaking, eye to eye,
> Though, lip with lip, they may not feed delight.

[1] p. 4.   [2] Ibid. 51.

The jealous have no wit to interpose
In that eye-converse, whatsoe'er they do,
Our lips are silent and the watchers doze,
And eye to eye has passed the message true.
Dear, read my eyes across the jealous throng
There in your corner: 'Keep this night for me,
Curse on the loveless nights that do us wrong,
Shut out the morn, curtain the night with thee.'
Mary! slim queen of poets, hear my cry:
Fie on last night that sped so swiftly by!

How and where were these poems written? There is no internal evidence, and the external evidence is scanty and difficult of interpretation. But we can make a reasonable guess which will not be altogether wide of the mark. So far as they are the product of the bards they were probably written under the bardic conditions, somewhat relaxed no doubt for verse which was a little apart from the professional stock in trade of the poets and need not conform to the more rigid rules of the art. While the schools lasted it was the custom—a custom of immemorial antiquity—to compose in the dark. The poets 'tossing on their beds' (to use Mr. Yeats's phrase in another connexion) ordered the lines of their verses and disposed their assonances and alliterations in 'a chamber deaf to noise and blind to light'. This was their day's portion, and in the evening candles were brought into the main chamber of the school and the poems were written down to be submitted to the searching technical criticism of the master. From the metrical tracts which have come down to us we can see how intense a scrutiny they had to undergo. And to this training these verses owe their clean idiom and the concinnity of their technique.

But were they fashioned thus? We cannot tell. There are many alternatives, and of those many I like to fancy that one hits the mark. Professor Bergin has translated a poem from the Book of O'Conor Don, in which a poet of the stricter school attacks an errant bard for making his poems on horseback riding over the hills. There is no reason why poems should not be composed on horseback (Swinburne did it), but to the bardic mind it seemed a wanton break with sacred tradition. Yet these poems of light love made by nobles as well as bards may well have been dictated by a Muse that

> Tempered her words to trampling horses' feet
> More oft than to a chamber-melody.

If Sir Philip Sidney made his sonnets on the highway, so may our poets, his analogues in Ireland, have 'reined their rhymes into buoyant order' on the mountain roads. At any rate, if we indulge this fancy, there is none that can disprove it.

Well, however composed, they have been preserved for our delight. And we may spend a little more time in considering their nature. We have seen already that their chief marks are beauty and irony—beauty to lend them wings, and irony to keep those wings from soaring too high. A love poetry that studies beauty alone readily degenerates into sentiment. But these were born before the days of sentiment and keep the detachment and the realism of that older and wiser world. They have little psychology—one of the modern forms of inverted sentiment—and, for the most part, conceive woman with an enviable simplicity as beautiful and false. This is a part of the old Provençal tradition, in which no woman was ripe for love until she was married and few were allowed to commit the indiscretion of loving a husband. And so it is rare to find a husband speaking of a wife in these poems. There is one piece which I know from only one manuscript (Eg. 155 in the British Museum), in which a husband grieves because his wife has left him. There is no doubt that the word *tréigbhedil* used in the heading implies a voluntary desertion on the part of the wife. For whom had she left him? It would be natural to assume a mortal lover, and, read so, the husband's praise would bear witness to a touching loyalty in another's disloyalty. It seems to me possible, however, to suppose the lover with whom she had gone from him to be Death. In that case the word would convey a gentle reproach to be paralleled by that lovely poem of Coventry Patmore's:

> It was not like your great and gracious ways.
> Do you that have nought other to lament,
> Never, my Love, repent
> Of how, that July afternoon,
> You went,
> With sudden, unintelligible phrase,
> And frightened eye,
> Upon your journey of so many days,
> Without a single kiss, or a goodbye?

If this interpretation seem fanciful, the poem is printed here, and the reader is free to choose between the alternatives.

Moladh mná ré n-a fear tar éis a thréigbheála

> Dá ghealghlaic laga leabhra,
> troighthe seada sítheamhla,
> dá ghlún nach gile sneachta,—
> rún mo chridhe an chuideachta.

> Trillse drithleacha ar lonnradh,
> taobh seang mar sról . . .
> braoithe mar ruainne rónda,
> gruaidhe naoidhe neamhónda.

> Ní thig díom a chur i gcéill
> díol molta dá dreach shoiléir,
> stuagh leanbhdha mhaordha mhálla
> mheardha aobhdha éadána.

D'éis gach radhairc dá bhfuair sinn
do mhearaigh go mór m'intinn
   ná raibhe suan i ndán damh;
   is truagh mo dhál im dhúsgadh.

Dob usa gan éirghe dhamh
d'fhéachaint an tighe im thiomchal;
   ní bhfuair sinn a sompla ó shoin,
   inn fá dhocra 'na deaghaidh.

Some of the beauty and tenderness of this poem may
survive into an English version.

He praises his wife when she has left him

White hands of languorous grace,
Fair feet of stately pace
And snowy-shining knees—
My love was made of these.

Stars glimmered in her hair,
Slim was she, satin-fair;
The straight line of her brows
Shadowed her cheek's fresh rose.

What words can match her ways,
That beauty past all praise,
That courteous, stately air,
Winsome and shy and fair.

To have known all this and be
Tortured with memory—
Curse on this waking breath—
Makes me in love with death.

Better to sleep than see
This house now dark to me
A lonely shell in place
Of that unrivalled grace.

The ladies celebrated in these poems are beautiful after
one pattern, the bright-haired type always admired where
a population is mixed of dark and fair. Under golden

tresses, rippled or in innumerable curls, shines the broad white forehead, luxuriant brows shade blue eyes moving in their orbit with a stately slowness, the cheeks smoulder like a fire, the lips are crimson over the level range of snowy teeth, the neck is straight and slender, the bosom is white as fresh-fallen snow or the foam of the sea, the wave of breast and side and knee flows beautifully down to the straight calves and trim white feet, that bear up all this lovely weight—the details of this picture appear again and again in these poems, and only one writer, Richard Burke, confesses his love for any and every type of beauty, so that it be willing and his own.

To such beauty our poets are infinitely, though perhaps not too seriously, susceptible. And their love, too, is of the old tradition. It is a sweet sickness—that bitter-sweet which the poets of the Greek anthology already knew; it must be hidden from jealous watchers and spoken only in the eyes, it haunts them in their waking hours, and, 'like a jewel hung in ghastly night', it will not leave them when they sleep; death is their only refuge from it, and when they die it will stand between them and God's love. And now and again a mocking voice strikes in and blows all this light and glittering web of make-believe into the air. 'Death is all your desire,' it says; 'die then, but leave all the women behind for me, the sole survivor of the slaughter. You are sick with love; I, too, love, but I keep my health. The world of your disordered fancies is still the old familiar world to me.' So the argument proceeds, and they spend all their long-meditated art in the elaboration of casuistical subtleties: they are dead, but their ghosts keep up a semblance of life about the place where love murdered them; they envy the blind, secure from the basilisk glance of fatal beauty; their hearts are at issue with the eyes that let in the lovely shafts that pierced them through; they are miserable, but their misery is their sole delight—and in the midst of all this suffering they are never so lost that they cannot formulate a paradox or give a fresh turn to some one of the ancient conceits.

For like all poetry of the kind, these verses are profoundly literary, full of reminiscence and suggestion of other times and literatures. One stanza recalls that famous and much-imitated dialogue, the ninth ode of Horace's third book:

> Donec gratus eram tibi,
>> Nec quisquam potior bracchia candidae
> Cervici iuvenis dabat,
>> Persarum vigui rege beatior.

Surely this was in the mind of the man who wrote in just such a dialogue:

> Do b'fhearr liom it fhochair-se,
>> ós duit tugas mo chéadchais,
> inás ríghe an domhain-se
>> do bheith agam it éagmhais.[1]

Cearbhall Ó Dálaigh's echo-song brings us into another world, the world of the Renaissance, for the Elizabethans borrowed from Italy that device of the mocking echo which John Webster used with such strange effect in *The Duchess of Malfi*. And when we read Pierce Ferriter:

> Foiligh oram do rosg rín,
>> má théid ar mharbhais dínn leat;
> ar ghrádh th'anma dún do bhéal,
>> ná feiceadh aon do dhéad gheal,[2]

our own lips begin to move involuntarily and to murmur:

> Take, oh, take those lips away,
>> That so sweetly were forsworn;
> And those eyes, the break of day,
>> Lights that do mislead the morn.

[1] 'I would rather be with you, since you are my first love, than to be king of all the world without you'; O'Rahilly, *Dánta Grádha*, 20.

[2] 'Hide your bright eyes, if you are pardoned after having slain so many: on your life do not open your lips, lest those shining teeth be seen'; ibid. 34.

Ó Géaráin bids his mistress put away her mirror lest, looking in it, she herself be lost for love of all that irresistible
beauty and pine away self-slain like Narcissus. So the
Shropshire Lad, in our own day, warns his love:

> Look not in my eyes, for fear
> They mirror true the sight I see;

and for fear that she also will dote upon her image, like
Narcissus who now wavers in the wind 'a jonquil, not a
Grecian lad'. We might go on matching thought with
thought, image with image, pain with pain, out of that
age-long Book of Love, whose pages return always upon
themselves, so that the poets of the Greek anthology, the
Romans Ovid and Propertius, the men of Provence, their
pupils of Italy, the Elizabethans, the Jacobeans, the
Carolines, write in again and again the same things with
every variety of script and idiom.

And yet when we had finished our comparisons, we
should find that there was something unconquerably native
and original in the Irish contributions, an inbred tone and
quality that comes from another tradition than the common European and that gives their peculiar edge and
accent to these poems. This is more to be felt than illustrated, and it cannot be conveyed to those who do not
know the language, for, as with all good poetry, here, too,
the whole effect is dependent upon the deft handling of
idiom and a keen sense of the history and the associations
of words. And one who has attempted the translation of
certain of these poems may be allowed to think that it is
something more than an apology for failure to claim that
they are essentially untranslatable. This native quality
does not come altogether from their use of the figures of
Irish story to point their argument, as when one poet, per-
suading his unwilling mistress to fly with him, recites the
many precedents of elopement among the heroines of

legend, or another celebrates the inventors of the arts of love among the Gael, telling with a pleasant fancy how Naoise discovered kissing one evening when he found Deirdre drawing on her trews, and how it has been left for him, the poet, to open the doors of jealousy, and now, alas! he cannot close them. No, it is a deeper thing than that, a something essential dyed in the material that makes them strange and singular in their kind. There could be no better illustration of this than that remarkable poem first printed by Dr. E. J. Gwynn, put into the mouth of the wife of Aodh Ó Ruairc, whom Thomas Costello is besieging with love in her husband's absence.[1] It is a picture of a woman swaying between two loves, and many such pictures have been drawn, but never one like this. The poem divides itself into two halves, each of sixteen quatrains, the first half addressed to the husband, the second to the lover, only the lover has the lodgement of half a quatrain in the husband's portion. This distribution of the quatrains is in itself an exact image of the woman's mind. For she is going upon the razor edge of love; a nothing, a breath, a feather, a snowflake, two lines of verse, would incline her this way or that; she is faithful to her husband, yet as she wavers on the debatable border her mind has already passed over and waits for her body to follow; she calls to her husband to save her from all the subtle arts of her poet lover, and then turns to the lover and, pouring out her uncontrollable passion in a flood of wild apostrophes that leave no veil upon her secret will, she bids him betake him to his art of poetry and spare her and her husband and their wedded love. All this is told in an idiom of perfect simplicity, only the verse has all the complex harmony of alliteration and assonance and consonance that lends so subtle a charm to that most Irish of measures, the *deibhidhe*. The poem is in essence what Browning used to call a dramatic lyric, and is the last

[1] *Ériu*, ix. 1; *Dánta Grádha*, 55.

in a long series of poems, like the 'Old Woman of Beare' and 'Liadain and Cuirithir', in which a figure or a situation of passion is realized with an absolute and final intensity. Such poems as these would alone justify the study of Irish literature, for their like is not to be found elsewhere, and their disappearance would be a loss, not only to Ireland, but to the whole world.

When Edmund Spenser was discoursing with his friend Eudoxus, the interlocutor questioned the poet on the compositions of the 'kinde of people called the bardes, which are to them insteade of Poetts': 'Tell me, I pray you,' said he, 'have they any arte in their composicons? or bee they any thinge wyttye or well favored as poems shoulde bee?' 'Yea, truly,' answered Spenser,

I haue caused diuers of them to be translated unto me, that I might understande them, and surelye they savored of sweete witt and good invencon, but skilled not of the goodly ornamentes of Poetrie; yet were they sprinckled with some prettye flowers of theire owne naturall devise, which gave good grace and comlines unto them, the which yt is great pittye to see soe good an ornament abused, to the gracinge of wickednes and vice, which woulde with good usage serve to bewtifie and adorne virtue.

There are translations and translations. And we do not know who served Spenser in this office. It is clear that the poems he meant were bardic poems of the more formal sort extolling the deeds of chiefs. Poems of our type, perhaps, never came his way. Surely, if they had, he would have recognized a familiar note in them. For these poems are witty and well favoured in a kind that was only being brought to perfection in England in Spenser's own day. In the days when English bards were busy in beautifying and adorning the virtue of Henry VIII, this style was first practised in England. And that first harvest was gathered into the collection known from its printer as *Tottel's Mis-*

cellany in 1557. The most casual glance at that volume will show how closely akin in subject these productions of the society that gathered round the Earl of Surrey and Sir Thomas Wyatt are to the Irish poems here printed. A few examples will suffice to show this. The examples may be taken from Sir Thomas Wyatt the Elder.

To a ladie to answere directly with yea or nay

Madame, withouten many wordes:
Once I am sure, you will, or no.
And if you will, then leaue your boordes,
And vse your wit, and shew it so.

For with a beck you shall me call.
And if of one, that burns alway,
Ye have pity, or ruth at all:
Answer hym fayer with yea, or nay.

If it be yea: I shall be faine.
Yf it be nay: frendes as before.
You shall another man obtain:
And I mine owne, and yours no more.

And here is a rendering by Wyatt of a *strambotto* of Serafino's:

To his love whom he had kissed against her will

Alas, Madame, for stealing of a kisse,
Haue I so much your mynde therein offended?
Or haue I done so greuously amisse:
That by no meanes it may not be amended?
Reuenge you then, the rediest way is this:
Another kisse my life it shall haue ended.
For, to my mouth the first my heart did suck:
The next shall clene out of my brest it pluck.

The Irish poems are collaterals descended from a common ancestor, but by a different way. Surrey and Wyatt got their inspiration out of Italy; it is a probable conjecture that our Irishmen derived the matter of their art from

French sources, though in the later stages an English influence is certainly to be reckoned with.

But there is one main difference between the two schools. Reading *Tottel*, one is conscious of a matter not entirely assimilated, of a style as yet uncertain of achievement. Fine though much of the poetry is, it is yet not sure of itself, it lacks the poise and balance of achieved lyric art. That was to come later with Sir Philip Sidney and his fellows. In the Irish it is otherwise. The highest flights of the company of Surrey are above the reach of our poets. But the least remarkable of these Irish poems shows no lapse in technique, nothing otiose or unnecessary in style. Every word has its place and its meaning. The rhyming is perfect, the expression always neat and epigrammatic. These are not, as Spenser ignorantly affirmed, the 'pretty flowers of their own natural device', an accidental blundering into beauty, but rather 'the goodly ornaments of poetrie', the fruit of a long training and of old tradition.

The question of tradition is the gist of the whole matter. There was not in Surrey's day a stable tradition in English verse in poetry of this kind. In Ireland, on the other hand, an old and honoured tradition gave the poets a firm and steady grasp of style. One may quote here the excellent words of W. P. Ker in his address on 'The Eighteenth Century' to the English Association:

It is the convention of a school or a tradition, such as keeps the artists from eccentricity, vanity, and 'expense of spirit', the convention which makes an understanding between them as to what is worth doing, and sets them speedily to work, instead of wasting their time considering what they ought to do next.

This is said of the convention of the English eighteenth century, but it is equally true of the Irish poetical convention while it was still practised by the trained bards. In the eighteenth century the real life went out of the convention, and a diffuse and formless style replaced the strict athletic manner of the bards. But our poets still stand on the ancient ways, and their admirable idiom shows us the Irish speech as a living and muscular organism, producing literature.

VII

THE END OF THE TRADITION

TOWARDS the end of the sixteenth century the constant state of devastating war in Ireland, the pitiful results of which have been described for Munster by Edmund Spenser, had begun to affect the patronage which was the necessary background of the bardic order as I have described it. In a manuscript from Tipperary of about 1600, written for one of the old English family of Butler, a poet addressing a lady of that family deplores the decay of the old generosity to the poets:[1]

> Ah! liberal-handed lady, though
> Round Éire's shore the generous wave
> Ebbs now, in thee 'tis still at flow;
> No marvel that the bard's thy slave.
>
> A lady passionate for song,
> True friend of all the bardic kind,
> Who cleaves to her can scarce go wrong;
> Song to her loaned doth interest find.
>
> The good tradition holds no more
> Of open-handedness to art;
> On later manners men set store
> And close their purse-strings and their heart.
>
> Now that the giving spirit's gone
> And wealth and art are by the ears,
> That poet's mad who labours on
> And gives to song his wasted years.
>
> In ancient Ulster as of old
> Dwelt Liberality of right;
> Now Ulster hearts are changed and cold,
> From all that province she takes flight.

[1] See Flower, *Catalogue*, 6, § 20.

> She's chased from Munster; Connacht too
> Gives her no welcome as of yore;
> The hapless hunger-stricken crew
> Know Liberality no more.

> She's known no more where the wide plain
> Of Leinster spreads beneath the skies;
> Unless another shape she's ta'en,
> That hides her from the poet's eyes.

> A mist has caught her from our sight,
> A druid mist that hides her o'er;
> Ask but a lodging for the night
> And all men turn you from the door.

By the beginning of the seventeenth century Ireland lay exhausted and panting, and what seemed the final blow to all her hopes and to the old order of things under which the poets had flourished was dealt by the mysterious flight of the two northern earls, Tyrone and Tyrconell, in 1607, an event that led directly to the Plantation of Ulster under the deputy Chichester, and as an inevitable result to the rising of 1641. The two earls were to die in exile, Tyrconell the following year and Tyrone eight years later. It is said that, as the ship that carried them away set sail down Loch Swilly, a great cry of lament and farewell went up from their followers left behind upon the shore. One of their poets has expressed all that this fateful moment meant for those to whom the old Irish order was the only way of life they had known and who were now to see that order crumbling into ruins about them:[1]

> This night sees Éire desolate,
> Her chiefs are cast out of their state;
> Her men, her maidens weep to see
> Her desolate that should peopled be.

[1] Knott, *Ériu*, viii. 191; Walsh, *Catholic Bulletin*, xviii. 1074.

How desolate is Connla's plain,
Though aliens swarm in her domain;
Her rich bright soil had joy in these
That now are scattered overseas.

Man after man, day after day
Her noblest princes pass away
And leave to all the rabble rest
A land dispeopled of her best.

O'Donnell goes. In that stern strait
Sore-stricken Ulster mourns her fate,
And all the northern shore makes moan
To hear that Aodh of Annagh's gone.

Men smile at childhood's play no more,
Music and song, their day is o'er;
At wine, at Mass the kingdom's heirs
Are seen no more; changed hearts are theirs.

They feast no more, they gamble not,
All goodly pastime is forgot,
They barter not, they race no steeds,
They take no joy in stirring deeds.

No praise in builded song expressed
They hear, no tales before they rest;
None care for books and none take glee
To hear the long-traced pedigree.

The packs are silent, there's no sound
Of the old strain on Bregian ground.
A foreign flood holds all the shore,
And the great wolf-dog barks no more.

Woe to the Gael in this sore plight!
Henceforth they shall not know delight.
No tidings now their woe relieves,
Too close the gnawing sorrow cleaves.

These the examples of their woe:
Israel in Egypt long ago,
Troy that the Greek hosts set on flame,
And Babylon that to ruin came.

Sundered from hope, what friendly hand
Can save the sea-surrounded land?
The clan of Conn no Moses see
To lead them from captivity.

Her chiefs are gone. There's none to bear
Her cross or lift her from despair;
The grieving lords take ship. With these
Our very souls pass overseas.

If their souls passed overseas the bodies of many of them
were soon to follow. For, as the plantations proceeded and
the Irish nobility were reduced to poverty, a tide of emigration began, the forerunner of the Flight of the Wild Geese
after the fall of Limerick and the great emigration after the
famine. It was impossible for Catholics to get higher education in Ireland, and after picking up what elementary
education they could in the little schools in the towns, or
in the bardic seminaries which still survived in a shrunken
form, they were forced to go abroad to Salamanca or
Rome, to Paris or Bordeaux, to Douai or Louvain. Thus
Geoffrey Keating, the historian, studied at Bordeaux and
returned to Ireland to lurk in the hills of Tipperary and
gather from the manuscripts of the MacEgans the material
for his *Forus Feasa ar Éirinn*. For, as the darkness gathered
over Ireland, the poets and scholars turned again to the
past and set themselves to gather up once more the long-
meditated antiquities of their country which were now
threatened with final destruction. This has always seemed
to me to provide the explanation of that curious collection
of poems known as the Contention of the Bards. It has
often been made a matter of reproach to the poets that in
this hour of desperate need they revived once more the

ancient rivalry between north and south and, as a contemporary expressed it in a bitter epigram, wrangled over the kennel when the whelps had been stolen. But this was not in their intention. They desired to set on record once more the ancient historical and genealogical learning, and they chose the traditional method of a contention, setting out the glories of the past in a kind of antiphony of learning.

A more remarkable enterprise was undertaken at Louvain. Here in the college dedicated to St. Anthony of Padua, founded by Florence O'Mulconry, a member of one of the most famous families of historians in Ireland, the Franciscan friars and the poets gathered and addressed themselves to the task of committing to print all the antiquities of Ireland. The inspiration came, perhaps, from Bollandus, who had already begun upon that vast compilation of the Lives of the Saints which is still in process of publication at Brussels by the Society named after him. Under the leadership of Ward and Colgan, both members of great poetic families of the north, they planned to put to the press the lives of the saints, the annals of Ireland, and all the miscellaneous antiquities bequeathed to them by the faithful labours of so many generations of clerics, poets, and scholars. Transcripts were to be made of all important manuscripts, and from these copies, concentrated at Louvain, a stately series of printed volumes was to be drawn to preserve the record for all posterity. Only a portion of this great scheme came to fruition. The first volume of the lives of the saints and the *Trias Thaumaturga*, a copious collection of material for the biography of Saints Patrick, Bridget, and Columcille, were printed. The other collections remained in manuscript. The most active collaborator in this enterprise was the poor brother Michael O'Clery, who travelled throughout Ireland, assiduously transcribing wherever he went the darkened vellums which he found in the monasteries and in the castles of historians and lawyers and poets. Many of his copies still survive and they show that he did not limit himself to hagiological material, for many of the most fascinating poems of the older language were preserved by his accurate hand. O'Clery also compiled a new recension of the *Lebor Gabála*, the Book of Conquest, the ancient chronicle of early Irish history; and he and three others, members of the historian families of O'Clery, O'Mulconry, and O'Duignan, assembled what they could of the older monastic annals and digested them into a new collection, called after them *The Annals of the Four Masters*, which in the edition annotated by John O'Donovan is a main authority for Irish history. A press was set up at St. Anthony's and there, in a type modelled on the beautiful contemporary script, the first Irish books were printed, books of devotion designed to serve the needs of the hard-pressed Catholics of Ireland. Later in the century John O'Molloy issued at Rome his *Grammatica Hibernica*, a record of the practice of the Irish poetical schools. This attempt at the printing of Irish was to prove abortive, and it is a strange fact that of these first printed books more copies survive in manuscript than in the original form. The manuscript tradition reabsorbed these prints and went on continuously into our own time.

The streets of Louvain must have presented a strange spectacle at this time. The little university town was full of the Irish, friars and nobles and poets and scholars, jostling one another and exchanging the last news from home. Many poems written there still survive and show us to what straits the poets were reduced, shivering in poverty after the comfort and consideration which their art had always been able to buy for them in Ireland. At home the poets plunged deeper into destitution and despair. Their castles and lands were taken from them by the new conquerors, who could not understand how poetry could be a title to landed possessions. And since the sixteenth century they had been suspect as encouraging the local chieftains in their resistance to English rule and feeding their aristocratic pride by their eulogies and reminders of ancient glories. It is said that one of the MacBrodins, poets of Clare, was cast over a cliff by a Cromwellian soldier who cried after him as he fell: 'Sing your rann now, little man!' The whole history of this gradual degeneration of the poets can be read in the works of David O'Bruadair, who, born about 1625 and dying in 1698, saw the ruin of his country accomplished, and died in extreme poverty, still toiling at the transcription of manuscripts. His poems serve as a kind of running commentary on the events of that terrible century, and in them we can see, through the antique dress of a style still clinging to the old traditions of the schools, all the feelings of the men who watched the rising in 1641, the Cromwellian fury, the short reign in Ireland of James II, the battle of the Boyne, the siege of Athlone, Aughrim, and the fall of Limerick. His patrons gradually fell away and he was forced to labour with his hands like a hind:[1]

Here I am in hunger and thirst, a lonely labourer wielding a tool that I was not used to in my days of fulness. My knuckles are all swollen from the motion of the clay-spade, and its handle has completely ruined my fingers. Let not my distracted complaint move anyone to bring in his rashness any verdict of guilty against me; for it is not poverty that has caused half my sorrow, but my being worsted derisively by deceitful tricks in this crooked game of chess.

It was indeed a crooked game that fate and the world played against the blindfolded poets. They had been proud and wanton, and presumed often upon the privileges of their order. But now all that was gone and no man regarded them. They fell back in their despair on the one weapon left to them, that gift of satire and effective cursing inherited

[1] MacErlean, *Poems of David Ó Bruadair* (Irish Texts Society, London, 1910, 1913, 1916), i. xxviii = ii. 28, 30.

from the old enchanters, before which in the ancient days kings had trembled. One Peadar O'Mulconry writes a poem against a farmer in whose service he was, who had mocked his art of poetry:[1]

> Were not the Gael fallen from their high estate
> And Fola's warrior kings cast down by fate
> And learning mocked in Eire's evil day,
> I were no servant, Edmond, in thy pay.
>
> Ye shall not stay my toil, once held divine,
> Thou and thy fleering harlots at their wine,
> Till all the brave are dead and out of reach
> Eireamhon's people of the golden speech.
>
> Edmond, I give good counsel. Heed it thou!
> Leave mocking at my holy labours now,
> Or such a rain of venomed shafts I'll send
> That never a man shall save thee nor defend.
>
> A tale I've heard that well might tame thy mood.
> A gamesome chief of Gascony's best blood
> Refused a poet once. The satire sped
> And the man withered, strengthless, leprous, dead.

This poem is written in the new rhythmical form called by O'Bruadair, when compelled to condescend to it by the failure of the cultivated audience which could understand the subtle art of the old strict verse, *sráidéigse*, 'gutter poetry'. This was now to be the medium of Irish poetry and was to be chiefly practised in Munster and the district of south-east Ulster and north Leinster. And the cultivation of the old literary tradition became gradually limited to these areas. The tradition was still active in Connacht and Donegal through the seventeenth century, but it gradually failed there, and there are practically no manuscripts surviving from those districts in the eighteenth century. Folk-song and folk-tale abounded there, and by

[1] R.I.A. MS. F. V. 3, 212.

the sea and in the mountains the language held its ground until the present day, but so far as the tradition of the poets with which we have been dealing is concerned there is little of importance to be noted outside of the two chief areas of Munster and the Ulster–Leinster district. We have seen for more than ten centuries king, monk, and poet preparing and preserving that tradition the history of which is the true history of Irish literature. The poets shared in all their country's fortunes and fell with its fall. Of their glories and their triumphs I have endeavoured to give a faithful account. They had their faults, but of these they bought forgiveness with a song. And for an epilogue I take from a manuscript of their last days a metrical colophon in which the writer in his old age takes leave at once of love and of his twin arts of writing and of poetry:[1]

> Finis to all the manuscripts I've penned,
> And to life's fitful fever here an end,
> An end to lime-white women golden-tressed,
> And in God's hand at Judgement be the rest.

[1] O'Rahilly, *Búrdúin Bheaga*, 43.

REPRINTED LITHOGRAPHICALLY IN GREAT BRITAIN
AT THE UNIVERSITY PRESS, OXFORD
BY VIVIAN RIDLER
PRINTER TO THE UNIVERSITY